The Jiu- Jitsu Parent

A PRACTICAL GUIDE TO SUPPORTING YOUR CHILD'S JOURNEY

Philippe Eggert

Bali - Indonesia

Email: philippeeggert@gmail.com

Instagram: philippe_eggert

First published in 2025

Copyright © Philippe Eggert

Paperback ISBN: 979-8-89686-710-4

To Kris, my son—
Thank you for inspiring this journey
of growth, discovery, and love.
With all my heart, Paps..

ABOUT THE AUTHOR

Philippe Eggert is not just a Jiu-Jitsu dad—he's a passionate advocate for the sport and an active contributor to the Jiu-Jitsu community in Bali and Indonesia. As the Principal of Indonesia's first Youth National Jiu-Jitsu Team and the Technical Director of the inaugural ADCC Indonesian Open, he has actively contributed to the sport's growth in the region. Philippe also served as Head Marshal for the JJIF-JJAU Southeast Asia Regional Championship and has organized and supported numerous tournaments across the island. His dedication has made him a respected figure in the Indonesian BJJ community, where he supports the sport's development both locally and nationally.

Philippe is the Co-Founder of AoA—'Art of Alavanca,' a project focused on creating a premier Jiu-Jitsu retreat center and holistic elite training facility in Bali. As part of this initiative, he spearheaded the Jiu-Jitsu Performance Academy (JPA), a youth training and education program designed to inspire and nurture the next generation of athletes.

He is also the founder of Braus Fight Indonesia, which has made high-quality BJJ equipment accessible to practitioners across the country.

Philippe's personal Jiu-Jitsu journey began in 2018 at the age of 45. In 2023, he earned his purple belt at the age of 50 years. After more than a decade of supporting his son's Jiu-Jitsu adventure, Philippe continues to dedicate himself to the art and its community. Through his work, he strives to foster growth, development, and a deeper love for the 'Gentle Art.'

WHY JIU-JITSU MATTERS

Jiu-Jitsu is unlike anything else. It's not just a sport it is a martial art — it's a way of understanding life. At its heart, Jiu-Jitsu is about leverage, but not just the physical kind. It's the kind of leverage that teaches you how small, thoughtful adjustments can shift the balance in your favor. It's a philosophy, that persistence can overcome strength, that understanding beats force, and that there's always a solution — even when you feel stuck.

In today's world, that lesson matters more than ever. Life moves fast, and it's easy to feel overwhelmed, distracted, disconnected, and caught in a cycle of reacting. Jiu-Jitsu slows everything down and connects you to the moment. It forces you to focus, to breathe, to solve problems when they appear. On the mats, you can't fake effort, and you can't avoid challenges. Every roll is a mirror, showing you your limits, your mistakes, but also revealing how much more you're capable of. It's not about ego—it's about growth. And every time you face that mirror, you learn a little bit more about yourself.

What makes Jiu-Jitsu special, it is for everyone. It doesn't matter where you're from, how old you are, or what you've been through. The mats are a place where we're all equal—where effort and respect are the only currencies that matter. This inclusivity builds something rare in today's world, a genuine sense of loyalty and trust. In a room full of strangers, you'll find people who challenge you, support you, and celebrate your progress. That kind of connection goes beyond technique—it changes how we see and treat each other.

And the lessons don't stop there. Jiu-Jitsu has this way of infiltrating into the rest of your life. It teaches discipline without rigidity, humility without weakness, and problem-solving without panic. It shows you how to embrace struggle, how to lose without giving up, and how to keep going when things feel impossible. These lessons aren't just for athletes—they're for kids, students, bankers, janitors, engineers, farmers, nerds, nurses, soldiers… becoming friends. Jiu-Jitsu builds better humans, this is what I sincerely believe.

In many ways, Jiu-Jitsu is a reflection of life itself. It's not linear; it's messy, full of setbacks, breakthroughs, and moments of clarity. But through all of that, it teaches us to keep showing up. To keep moving forward. To keep learning. And I know that if more people embraced these principles, we'd see a better, more connected world.

This is why Jiu-Jitsu matters. It's not about belts, trophies, or ranks—it's about growth. It's about becoming the kind of person who understands the value of struggle, who learns to connect through respect, and who carries those lessons into every aspect of life.

WHY YOUR ROLE MATTERS

Every parent wants to give their child the best possible start in life—the tools to face challenges, the confidence to pursue their passions, and the resilience to overcome setbacks. Jiu-Jitsu offers all of this and more. It's not just a combat sport; it's a powerful way to help children grow into well-rounded, confident, and capable individuals.

By introducing your child to Jiu-Jitsu, you're opening the door to something truly transformative. On the mats, they'll learn more than techniques—they'll learn how to face struggles with grit and determination. They'll encounter challenges that demand problem-solving, adaptability, and perseverance. Over time, they'll grow stronger—not just physically, but mentally and emotionally.

In a world where instant gratification often overshadows the value of hard work, Jiu-Jitsu stands out. It's a place where kids learn patience and the importance of consistent effort. It's where they'll face failure and frustration but also experience the joy of progress and the satisfaction that comes with earned success. Few activities build character as effectively.

As a parent, your role is essential. You're the one who opens this door, encouraging them to try, supporting them when they stumble, and celebrating their victories—big and small. You don't need to know anything about Jiu-Jitsu to make this decision. All it takes is believing in the value of helping your child grow through meaningful challenges.

Jiu-Jitsu isn't just about making kids stronger; it's about helping them become better humans. It teaches respect—for themselves, their peers, and the process of learning. It fosters discipline, focus, and accountability. Most importantly, it builds resilience, showing kids they can rise no matter how many times they fall.

Choosing Jiu-Jitsu for your child means giving them more than an activity—it's giving them a foundation for life. The values they develop on the mats— confidence, humility, perseverance, and respect—will stay with them long after childhood. In a constantly changing world, these qualities truly matter.

So why Jiu-Jitsu? Because it's more than a sport— it's a gift that will shape who they are and who they become. And your role in this journey? It's to help them take that first step and be there every step of the way.

"Give a child Jiu-Jitsu,

and you give them the tools

to face life with courage,

humility, and strength."

- Philippe Eggert

FOREWORD BY CLARK GRACIE

Dear Reader,

It's an honor to contribute to this book and to speak directly to parents who are embracing the incredible journey of Jiu-Jitsu alongside their children. Watching kids grow through Jiu-Jitsu is one of the most rewarding experiences I've had as both a practitioner and an instructor. Philippe has beautifully captured what makes this journey so special—not just for the child but for the entire family.

Meeting Philippe in Bali years ago, I could feel his passion for the art. His enthusiasm wasn't just about the technical side of Jiu-Jitsu; it was about how the practice changes lives. As I've seen firsthand, Philippe's dedication as a Jiu-Jitsu parent has been inspiring. His work has brought people together, fostered growth, and created opportunities for so many—especially young athletes.

This book isn't written by someone observing from the sidelines. Philippe is in the trenches—training, learning, and growing alongside his son. He knows the joys and challenges that come with supporting a young athlete because he's lived them. He also understands the profound impact Jiu-Jitsu can have, not just on the child wearing the gi but on the entire family.

What I love most about Philippe's perspective is how deeply he connects Jiu-Jitsu to life. It's not about medals or trophies; it's about the lessons of resilience, humility, and respect that extend far beyond the mats. These are lessons that strengthen bonds, deepen connections, and shape lives in ways few other activities can.

Philippe's story is a testament to how Jiu-Jitsu touches lives far beyond the training room. His insights, drawn from years of experience, offer a heartfelt guide for families entering this world. Whether you're just starting out or have been on this path for a while, this book will remind you why Jiu-Jitsu is so much more than what happens on the mats.

Thank you for taking the time to support your child in this journey. By doing so, you're giving them the tools to thrive—not just in Jiu-Jitsu but in life. And for that, I'm honored to stand alongside you and Philippe in sharing this message.

With respect and gratitude, **Clark Gracie**

Let yourJiu Jitsu Flow

- Clark Gracie -

FOREWORD BY THE AUTHOR

Dear Parent,

Thank you for picking up this book—it's a testament to the love and care you have for your child's growth and well-being.

In these pages, I want to share my experiences, struggles, and the lessons I've learned—through trial and error—as a Jiu-Jitsu dad. I'm not a psychologist or a professional coach, just a parent who loves his son and is enjoying his own Jiu-Jitsu journey.

Over the past decade, I've had countless conversations with other parents. We've shared the emotional rollercoaster of competitions, the uncertainty of making the right decisions, and the joy of watching our kids grow and entertain us with their playfulness. Parenting is an ever-changing challenge. Each age brings new surprises and forces us to adapt on the fly. It's a journey filled with frustrations and joys, with no perfect roadmap—just our honest intentions and the willingness to grow alongside our children.

Jiu-Jitsu has a unique way of touching lives. It's not just a sport or martial art—it's a journey of self-discovery, growth, and transformation. When I first stepped onto the mat, I had no idea how much it would change me. But perhaps the most rewarding part of my journey has been watching my child experience those same lessons and challenges, growing not just as a practitioner but as a person.

To truly understand what your child is experiencing, I wholeheartedly recommend putting on a Gi and giving Jiu-Jitsu a try yourself. Training alongside your son or daughter builds a bond of trust and respect that few other activities can offer. Even one class can give you a new perspective and deepen your connection to what your child is learning and achieving.

This book is the guide I wish I had when my family first began this journey. Whether you're new to the world of Jiu-Jitsu or have been supporting your child for years, I hope it will offer insight, inspiration, and practical advice as you walk this path together.

Thank you for being an amazing parent. Embrace the process, and approach each challenge with curiosity and patience.

With gratitude,
Philippe

TABLE OF CONTENTS

Introduction
Why Jiu-Jitsu for Kids?

PART A:
AGE-SPECIFIC DEVELOPMENT

PART B:

GENERAL PRINCIPLES OF BEING A SUPPORTIVE PARENT

(Focus: Broader Guidance for All Ages)

PART C:

SUPPORTING YOUTH ATHLETES

Introduction:

When Kris first stepped onto the Jiu-Jitsu mat, I didn't realize how much it would transform not just his life but mine as well.

As parents, we strive to give our children the best possible opportunities to grow, thrive, and develop the skills they need to navigate life's challenges. Jiu-Jitsu offers exactly that—a safe yet demanding environment where kids learn resilience, discipline, and respect while having fun along the way.

But let's be honest—being a Jiu-Jitsu parent isn't always easy. From finding the right gym to navigating tournament nerves, balancing school schedules, and handling those moments when your child wants to quit, the journey can feel overwhelming. That's exactly why I wrote this guide: to help you navigate the challenges and embrace the rewards of supporting your child's Jiu-Jitsu journey.

THE PARENT'S ROLE IN
A CHILD'S JIU-JITSU JOURNEY

Your support—emotional, logistical, and motivational—shapes how your child grows, faces challenges, and finds joy in their practice. Are they motivated to give their best effort, or do they feel overwhelmed by expectations? Are they learning resilience from setbacks, or are they discouraged by failure? Your role is about more than cheering from the sidelines—it's about being the steady, encouraging presence they can rely on.

I wrote this book because I've been there. I've watched my child's confidence grow on the mat, but I've also faced moments of frustration, doubt, and exhaustion as I tried to support his journey. This book isn't just about helping your child succeed in Jiu-Jitsu—it's about creating a partnership with them and the sport that fosters their strength, resilience, and readiness for life's challenges.

WHAT YOU'LL FIND IN THIS BOOK

Whether your child is taking their first steps on the mat or striving to become a champion, this guide will equip you with practical advice, age-specific insights, and tools to support them every step of the way. The book is structured into three parts:

Age-Specific Guidance: Understand and support your child as they grow through different stages of development—from playful beginners to self-driven teenagers.

General Principles for Supportive Parenting: Create a positive home environment, build trust with coaches, and find the balance between encouragement and pressure.

Supporting Youth Athletes: Help your child set realistic goals, handle competition pressure, and balance the demands of being both a young athlete and a growing individual.

You'll also find lessons from my own experiences as a parent, as well as insights gathered from world-class coaches and athletes I've meet over the years.

WHY THIS JOURNEY MATTERS

No matter where your family is on this journey, my goal is to help you approach it with confidence, patience, and the knowledge that you're not alone. Because at its core, Jiu-Jitsu is not about medals or promotions—it's about building better humans, one step at a time. As parents, we have the privilege of walking this transformative path alongside our children.

"It is not what you do

for your children,

but what you

have taught them

to do for themselves

that will make them

successful human beings."

- Ann Landers

LESSON LEARNED!

Before diving deeper into this book, I want to share a story—a lesson I learned the hard way.

Back when I was surfing every morning, we often went to the beach as a family. My wife and Kris would play in the sand while watching me surf. One day, after finishing a session, I approached the beach, and Kris—then about three years old—ran toward me through the knee-deep water. He grabbed my surfboard, eager to try it himself.

I helped him lay on the board and gave him a gentle push on a tiny wave toward the shore. He giggled and laughed, absolutely filled with joy. Then, determined and excited, he grabbed the board and tried pulling it back out to me. He wanted more!

This became our thing. Whenever I came out of the surf, he'd run to me, excited and ready to surf. He progressed quickly, starting to pop up and ride the little waves standing all the way to the beach. We had so much fun together. People on the beach would stop to watch, taking pictures of this tiny, fearless surfer. Comments like, "Oh, he's so talented!" or "This kid could be the next world champion!" made me feel so proud.

I started to see his potential. I believed he really could have a great future in the sport. So, I got him a custom-made tiny surfboard, perfectly shaped for him, and we dedicated specific surf sessions where I supported and coached him.

At first, he learned quickly, improving with every wave. I corrected his mistakes, adjusted his movements, and focused—with the best intentions—on helping him get better and better. We surfed for up to two hours at a time as often as possible. But slowly, things began to change.

He started repeating the same "mistakes" over and over again, and I began losing patience. I found myself yelling at him, frustrated that he wasn't doing things "right." He didn't seem as focused or as interested as before, and I told him he needed to take it more seriously and stop wasting the time I was giving him to learn.

Then one day, he looked at me and said, "Papi, can I go play sand? I don't want to surf."

That hit me hard. How could I refuse my 4-year-old such a simple request? I let him play in the sand that day, but after that, something changed. He never wanted to go surfing again. I tried everything—pressure, kindness, even manipulation—but nothing worked. His joy for surfing was gone, and I couldn't bring it back.

It hit me like a big wave crashing over my head: I had taken the most important thing about surfing away from him—his joy.

I realized then what an idiot I had been. My intentions were pure—I saw his potential, his talent, and the opportunities I thought I was creating for his future. But in my eagerness, I forgot something crucial: he was just a 4-year-old boy who needed to play, to explore the world with joy and curiosity.

When Kris started Capoeira after that, at age 4, and later joined a kids' Jiu-Jitsu class at 5, I approached things differently. I knew my number one priority as his parent was to keep his joy alive. I promised myself I would never again make his journey about my pride or how it made me feel.

Yesterday, Kris turned 15. He celebrated his birthday at the gym with his teammates, and it was wonderful. He spends about three hours a day on the mats, training hard and loving every moment. He's a Green-Black belt now, and his passion for Jiu-Jitsu shines through in how he shares his art with the little kids who look up to him.

All I did was step back. I kept my ego and pride out of his journey (not always successfully, I'll admit) and focused on keeping his love for what he was doing alive. That lesson has been one of the most important of my life, and it's one I carry with me every day as I support him in his journey.

I wanted to share this story with you because it highlights something every parent needs to remember: your child's journey is theirs, not yours. It's natural to feel pride in their accomplishments and want to help them succeed, but our role is to support them, not to take over their dreams or let our own expectations overshadow their joy.

As you guide your child through Jiu-Jitsu—or any activity—focus on nurturing their love for it. Protect their joy and curiosity, even when you see their potential and feel the urge to push. Let their journey be about discovery, growth, and happiness. And they will succeed!

"Our greatest gift

to our children is not

the path we pave for them,

but the joy we preserve

in their hearts

as they walk it."

— Philippe Eggert

Part A:
Age-Specific Development

INTRODUCTION

Every stage of a child's growth brings unique challenges and opportunities, shaped by the natural development of their brain. Understanding these phases can help us, as parents, provide the right kind of support and encouragement at the right time.

As children grow, their brains undergo rapid and remarkable changes, with each stage marked by specific cognitive, emotional, and social milestones. These changes not only influence how they learn and process information but also how they see the world and their role in it. By aligning our approach with their developmental needs, we can help them thrive—not just on the mats, but in every aspect of life.

THE EARLY YEARS (AGES 4-6)

During the early years, a child's brain is like a sponge, absorbing information at an astonishing rate. This phase is marked by rapid neural growth, particularly in the areas responsible for motor skills, language, and social interactions. At this age, play is the primary mode of learning. Activities that combine physical movement with fun—like Jiu-Jitsu—are especially beneficial, helping to build coordination, confidence, and the ability to work collaboratively with peers.

However, children in this stage have limited attention spans and are still developing emotional regulation. Success during these years doesn't come from perfection—it comes from creating a safe, playful environment where children feel encouraged to explore and make mistakes.

THE MIDDLE YEARS (AGES 7-10)

As children transition into their middle years, their brains enter a phase of synaptic pruning, where unused neural connections are eliminated, and frequently used ones are strengthened. This natural process enhances their ability to focus, solve problems, and retain new skills.

This is an ideal time to introduce more structure and consistency in training. At this stage, children begin to develop a deeper understanding of cause and effect, which helps them grasp the "why" behind techniques. However, these years are also marked by heightened sensitivity to feedback and peer dynamics. Building their confidence while fostering discipline and respect is key to supporting their growth.

THE PRETEEN YEARS (AGES 11-13)

Preteens experience significant brain growth, particularly in the prefrontal cortex—the area responsible for decision-making, planning, and self-regulation. At the same time, emotional processing, driven by the limbic system, often outpaces their ability to reason through situations calmly.

This phase marks the acceleration of both physical and emotional changes, presenting unique challenges. Preteens may begin setting personal goals and taking ownership of their journey, but they also need guidance to navigate the highs and lows of training. Keeping the fun alive while gradually introducing the concept of long-term commitment can help them stay engaged and motivated.

THE TEENAGE YEARS (AGES 14-16)

By the teenage years, the brain continues to refine its executive functions—such as impulse control, strategic thinking, and delayed gratification—though these abilities are still a work in progress. Adolescents are naturally drawn to independence and self-expression, and this is often when their passions begin to take shape.

For teenagers in Jiu-Jitsu, this stage can be transformative. They begin to take responsibility for their progress, explore leadership roles, and face competitive pressure. During this time, parents play a crucial role by stepping back to allow their teens to own their journey while remaining a steady source of support.

WHY AGE-SPECIFIC DEVELOPMENT MATTERS

Jiu-Jitsu is a sport that meets children where they are. By understanding the natural phases of brain development, it becomes easier to align support with their needs, helping them get the most from their training—whether it's building coordination as a young child, developing discipline and focus as they grow older, or learning resilience and independence as teenagers.

This section will guide you through these stages, offering insights into what children need most at each phase of their journey. Together, we'll explore how to help them thrive on the mats while growing into confident, capable individuals in every aspect of life.

"Parenting is not about shaping who our children will become, but about meeting them where they are and nurturing the unique potential that unfolds with each stage of their journey."
— *Philippe Eggert*

1. STARTING EARLY
(AGES 4-6):
THE FOUNDATION YEARS

The early years of a child's Jiu-Jitsu journey are all about exploration, fun, and building the foundations for a lifelong love of the Gentle Art. Kids at this age are naturally curious, energetic, and eager to learn. They live fully in the moment, which means their focus might shift quickly—but this also makes them incredibly adaptable and open to new experiences.

As a Jiu-Jitsu dad, I can tell you firsthand that these early years are about setting the stage, not chasing results. The goal is to create a positive, low-pressure environment where your child can explore, enjoy, and build confidence on the mat.

For me, this phase was a chance to sit back and simply enjoy the incredible entertainment of watching kids have fun. It became my favorite time to take my mind off work and responsibilities and embrace the joy of their playful energy. These moments were pure, filled with laughter and excitement, and they reminded me of the importance of keeping things light and enjoyable at this age.

LEARNING THROUGH PLAY

For kids aged 4 to 6, Jiu-Jitsu is all about discovering the joy of movement and play. At this stage, it's not about mastering techniques or competing—it's about building a strong foundation through fun. Coaches in good programs focus on games and activities that develop coordination, balance, and spatial awareness. These are the essential building blocks of Jiu-Jitsu, presented in ways that feel exciting and engaging for young minds.

As a parent, lean into this playful approach. Celebrate their natural enthusiasm for running, rolling, and learning how to move their bodies. This isn't the time to perfect techniques; it's about helping them experience the joy of Jiu-Jitsu in their own way.

BUILDING CONFIDENCE AND COORDINATION

Jiu-Jitsu at this stage is all about small victories that feel like big wins to your child. Watching them tumble, stand up, or escape from a position for the first time is a magical moment. It's not just about the technique—it's about seeing their confidence bloom as they realize, "I can do this!"

Your encouragement makes all the difference. Every time you cheer them on or tell them you're proud of their effort, you're showing them how much you believe in their ability to grow. Remember, their progress doesn't need to look like anyone else's—it's their journey, step by step, and every moment deserves celebration.

FINDING THE RIGHT GYM AND COACH

Choosing the right gym is critical, especially for young kids. Look for a program specifically designed for children, with coaches who are patient, fun, and skilled at working with this age group. A good children's class is one where kids are smiling, laughing, and excited to come back for the next session.

Take the time to visit a few gyms, observe classes, and talk to the coaches. As a Jiu-Jitsu dad, I learned how important it is to find a coach who treats the children with respect and makes learning enjoyable. A positive first experience with Jiu-Jitsu can set the tone for your child's entire journey, and the right coach will make all the difference.

MANAGING EXPECTATIONS

It's important to keep expectations realistic for this age. Most 4- to 6-year-olds are naturally curious and energetic, and it's completely normal for their focus to wander during class. At this stage, Jiu-Jitsu isn't about strict discipline or intense training—it's about having fun, staying active, and building foundational skills at their own pace.

As parents, it's easy to fall into the trap of expecting too much too soon. I've been guilty of it myself—wanting to see my child learn faster or take the sport more seriously. But the truth is, the journey needs to unfold at their pace. Encourage them, but let them lead the way. The focus should always be on enjoying the process, not rushing toward results.

PRACTICAL TIPS FOR PARENTS

Celebrate Small Wins: Did they complete a warm-up without getting distracted? Did they try a new move? Celebrate these moments, no matter how small they may seem.

Create a Routine: Consistency helps kids feel comfortable. Establish a regular schedule for classes, and turn it into a fun ritual they look forward to.

Stay Positive: Kids pick up on your energy. When you're excited and supportive, they're more likely to mirror that enthusiasm.

Be Patient: Progress might be slow, and that's perfectly normal. Avoid pushing too hard or expecting perfection—they're still little kids learning the basics of movement and coordination.

CONCLUSION FOR THIS AGE GROUP

The foundation years of Jiu-Jitsu are a time for exploration and growth, not pressure or performance. By fostering a love for the Art, encouraging play, and celebrating your child's unique journey, you'll help them build the confidence and coordination they need to thrive—both on and off the mat.

"Play is the highest form of research."

- Albert Einstein

2. GROWING PASSION
(AGES 7-10):
DEVELOPING SKILLS AND CONSISTENCY

By the ages of 7 to 10, Jiu-Jitsu begins to shift from play to purposeful practice. At this stage, children are not only growing physically but also developing intellectually. Their ability to process instructions, understand complex concepts, and think critically enhances their capacity to learn and apply techniques. This newfound mental sharpness allows them to connect with the principles of Jiu-Jitsu, discovering a genuine passion for learning and improvement. They're not just building strength and coordination—they're also learning the value of discipline, effort, and consistency in their training.

For parents, this phase is especially rewarding to witness. Watching a child's confidence grow with each new skill mastered is incredibly fulfilling. Their intellectual and physical development also means they're better equipped to recognize patterns, anticipate movements, and make strategic decisions —skills that serve them well in all areas of life. However, these years are pivotal in shaping their approach to commitment and resilience. The way parents guide and support their journey during this time can deeply influence their growth, both as athletes and as individuals.

DEVELOPING SKILLS:
ENCOURAGING CONSISTENCY

By this stage, Jiu-Jitsu becomes more than just a fun activity—it's an opportunity for your child to truly engage with the Art. They're learning to recognize patterns, understand techniques, and connect movement with strategy. Consistency is key at this point, as regular practice reinforces these skills and builds muscle memory.

Encourage your child to attend classes regularly, but keep the experience flexible and enjoyable. Remember, they're still kids, and their interest may naturally ebb and flow. The goal is to foster a habit of showing up—not to enforce a strict schedule. Creating a positive and consistent rhythm helps them see Jiu-Jitsu as an enjoyable, integral part of their life, rather than an obligation.

Practical Tip:

Turn skill-building into a game. After class, ask your child to "teach" you one thing they learned that day —whether it's a technique, a movement, or even something funny their coach said. This not only helps them retain what they've learned, but it also makes them feel proud and excited to share their progress with you.

BALANCING SCHOOL, SOCIAL LIFE, AND TRAINING

As children grow, their lives naturally become more dynamic. School demands increase, friendships deepen, and extracurricular activities start to fill their days. With so many priorities competing for their attention, it's important to ensure that Jiu-Jitsu remains a source of growth and joy, complementing their other interests without overwhelming them.

Helping your child create a balanced schedule allows for academic focus, social connection, and relaxation. Jiu-Jitsu should fit harmoniously into their life, adding value and enriching their experiences. Striking this balance ensures they continue to enjoy training while thriving in other areas.

Practical Tips:

Training Plan (Commitment) Encourage your child to talk with their coach about which classes best suit their goals and interests. Once they've chosen their sessions, help them commit by building a routine around those classes. This gives them a sense of ownership while ensuring their choices are supported by expert advice.

Weekly Game Plan Work together with your child to create a fun, colorful weekly schedule with stickers or visuals. Include time for Jiu-Jitsu, schoolwork, and their favorite activities. This not only teaches them the basics of time management but also makes their week feel enjoyable and balanced.

SUPPORTING THROUGH WINS AND LOSSES

At this stage, your child may begin participating in local tournaments, which can bring thrilling victories and the occasional emotional lows. Both are valuable parts of their journey, teaching lessons in perseverance, reflection, and respect.

One of the greatest lessons Jiu-Jitsu offers is the importance of respect and gratitude for opponents. Every match—whether it ends in triumph or a tough loss—is an opportunity for growth. Opponents are essential partners in progress; without them, there would be no competition, no challenges to overcome, and no chance to develop.

As a parent, your role is to guide your child through both the highs and the lows. Celebrate their courage in stepping onto the mat, and help them see that every match contributes to their growth. Whether they walk away with a medal or a meaningful lesson, they've gained something valuable.

Practical Tip:

After a tournament, acknowledge the effort they've put in and help them process the experience. For example, you might say, "You should be so proud of your effort out there. What did you enjoy most about the match?" or "I know that was tough—what's one thing you'd like to work on for next time?" This approach helps them see both victories and challenges as essential parts of their journey.

FOSTERING RESPECT AND DISCIPLINE

Respect and discipline don't just happen on the mat —they're cultivated through consistent actions and attitudes. By modeling respectful behavior yourself— such as supporting the coach's authority and encouraging sportsmanship—you reinforce the lessons they learn during training. This foundation shapes how they handle conflicts, setbacks, and successes, both in Jiu-Jitsu and in life.

Encourage your child to approach challenges with humility and view respect as a strength, not just a rule. These lessons don't just make them better athletes; they shape them into considerate, disciplined individuals who inspire those around them.

Practical Tip:

Bring the values they learn on the mat into everyday life. For example, if they're taught to bow before stepping onto the mat, encourage similar gestures of respect at home, like saying "please" and "thank you" or helping a sibling with a task. Reinforcing these habits shows that respect isn't just for training —it's a way of life.

PRACTICAL TIPS FOR PARENTS

Stay Engaged: Show genuine interest in your child's Jiu-Jitsu journey. Ask what they learned in class or watch their training sessions when possible. Your involvement reinforces how much you value their dedication.

Encourage Goal Setting: Help your child create small, achievable goals that build confidence, like mastering a new technique or earning their next stripe. These milestones keep them motivated and highlight the rewards of consistent practice.

Avoid Comparisons: Every child's journey in Jiu-Jitsu is unique. Celebrate your child's progress without measuring them against others. Focus on their individual growth and the joy they find in training.

Be Patient: Skill development takes time. Celebrate every step forward—whether it's landing a sweep for the first time or simply showing up with enthusiasm. Progress, no matter how small, is always worth acknowledging.

CONCLUSION FOR THIS AGE GROUP

By ages 7 to 10, children begin to see themselves as Jiu-Jitsu practitioners, not just participants. This phase is filled with growth, learning, and a deepening passion for the sport. By fostering consistency, balance, and respect, you're helping them build a strong foundation for success—both in Jiu-Jitsu and in life.

"Guide a child

with what engages

their mind and spirit,

not through force,

and you'll uncover

their true potential."

- Plato

3. STRENGTHENING COMMITMENT (AGES 11-13): NAVIGATING GROWTH AND KEEPING THE FUN ALIVE

The ages of 11 to 13 bring significant changes in your child's Jiu-Jitsu journey—and their life. Physically, they're gaining strength and coordination. Mentally, they're developing independence, analytical thinking, and a deeper ability to focus. This is a time when they begin making choices about their commitment to Jiu-Jitsu—whether it becomes a serious pursuit or remains a source of enjoyment and growth.

As parents, your role evolves during this stage. It's no longer just about encouraging participation—it's about guiding them through the unique challenges of adolescence. This phase is marked by self-discovery, growing responsibilities, and the need to keep their passion for Jiu-Jitsu alive. Your patience, presence, and understanding will help them navigate these changes while fostering a deeper connection to the Art.

PHYSICAL AND EMOTIONAL CHANGES IN PRETEENS

The preteen years are a time of transformation, both physically and emotionally. Growth spurts can affect coordination, while hormonal mood swings and shifting interests might make it harder for your child to stay motivated. These changes may sometimes show up on the mat as frustration or inconsistency in their performance.

This stage is all about patience—for both you and your child. Support them through "off" days and remind them that progress isn't always a straight path. Growth spurts may temporarily disrupt their balance or timing, but these are natural adjustments that come with growing up. Reassure them that the journey is about steady improvement, not perfection.

Practical Tips:

If your child feels uncoordinated or "off," remind them that their body is growing and adjusting—it's completely normal. Encourage them to focus on enjoying their time on the mats rather than worrying about getting everything right.

If mood swings or emotional outbursts happen, stay calm and supportive. Sometimes, just listening without trying to fix things can make a big difference. A simple, "It's okay, I'm here if you need me," lets them know they're not alone.

As Jiu-Jitsu begins to demand more focus and precision, it can sometimes feel overwhelming for kids. They might experience pressure from themselves, their coaches, or their peers. That's why it's essential to keep the joy of training at the forefront.

Remind your child that Jiu-Jitsu isn't just about accomplishments—it's about the fun of learning, the friendships they build, and the pride that comes from simply showing up. If you notice signs of stress or reluctance, take a step back and help them reconnect with what they love about the sport. Sometimes, a small change—like a new class format, a seminar, a private session, or even a short break— can reignite their enthusiasm.

Practical Tip:

Keep things fresh by encouraging your child to explore new aspects of Jiu-Jitsu, like trying No-Gi classes, experimenting with advanced techniques, or focusing on playful sparring sessions. Variety helps them stay engaged and reminds them why they fell in love with the sport in the first place.

HOW TO TALK TO
YOUR CHILD ABOUT GOALS

At this age, your child's ability to think critically about their goals begins to mature. Some may start dreaming of competing at higher levels, while others might prefer to enjoy Jiu-Jitsu as a hobby. Both paths are equally valid, and it's important to let your child take the lead in deciding what they want from the sport.

Keep the conversation open and supportive. Ask about their aspirations, and if they're aiming high, help them break those big dreams into smaller, actionable steps. For kids who aren't sure about their direction, reassure them that it's okay to train without a specific destination in mind. What matters most is that they're enjoying the journey.

Practical Tip:

If your child has a specific goal—like competing or mastering a technique—sit down together and create a simple plan to work toward it. Write it out, such as: "Focus on this sweep in your rolls" or, "Work on takedowns for the next tournament." Keep it visible at home as a reminder and a way to celebrate their progress.

Competition often becomes a bigger part of the Jiu-Jitsu experience at this age. Matches are longer, opponents are more skilled, and the stakes may feel higher. It's natural for your child to feel nervous or even uncertain about competing. These emotions are part of the process and provide an opportunity for growth.

As a parent, your role is to offer steady and positive support. Reinforce that competition is just one part of their Jiu-Jitsu journey, and encourage them to view each match as a chance to learn, regardless of the outcome. Celebrate their courage to compete, their sportsmanship, and their dedication—not just their victories.

Practical Tip:

Shift the focus to preparation rather than results. Of course, if they compete, they want to win. Help your child understand the importance of putting effort into training and trusting the process. Celebrate their bravery and hard work, no matter the outcome.

At this stage, kids begin to reflect more deeply on the values of Jiu-Jitsu and how it connects to their personal development. Respect and gratitude take on greater significance as they recognize the roles their coaches, teammates, and even opponents play in shaping their journey.

Teach your child to view every match and training session as a partnership. Opponents provide the challenges that help them grow, teammates offer motivation, and coaches provide invaluable guidance. Gratitude for these connections fosters humility, strengthens relationships, and creates a positive training environment.

Practical Tip:

Make gratitude a routine. Encourage your child to thank their coach, teammates, and even opponents after matches or training sessions. These small acts reinforce the values of mutual respect and appreciation.

Stay Involved: Preteens still need your support and presence. Ask about their training, watch their classes or matches, and celebrate their efforts. Your engagement shows them that their journey matters to you, and it's an opportunity to let them know how proud you are.

Keep Communication Open: Make time to talk with your child about how they're feeling—both physically and mentally. Be a safe space where they can share their thoughts without fear of judgment.

Encourage Balance: Help them manage their time effectively, ensuring they maintain a healthy mix of training, school, and downtime (*Body-Mind-Soul*). Learning balance now will benefit them for years to come.

Model Respect: Your actions set the tone. Show respect to their coaches, teammates, and even opponents, and your child will naturally follow your example.

CONCLUSION FOR THIS AGE GROUP

The preteen years can feel like a rollercoaster, filled with changes and challenges. But they're also a time of incredible growth, discovery, and development. By staying engaged, fostering open communication, and supporting your child with patience and encouragement, you're helping them build a strong, positive relationship with Jiu-Jitsu—and with you as their steady guiding force.

"Success is not

the key to happiness.

Happiness is

the key to success.

If you love

what you are doing,

you will be successful."

- Albert Schweitzer

4. MASTERY AND INDEPENDENCE (AGES 14-16): GUIDING TEENS TOWARD SELF-DRIVEN GROWTH

The teenage years mark a pivotal point in your child's Jiu-Jitsu journey. By ages 14 to 16, Jiu-Jitsu often becomes an integral part of their identity—not just as a sport, but as a way of life. Teens at this stage develop greater physical strength, sharper mental focus, and a deeper understanding of how techniques connect and unfold in detail. This combination often leads to significant progress on the mat. However, with these advancements come new challenges, including external pressures, self-doubt, and shifting priorities.

As parents, your role evolves into being a steady, supportive presence. It's about trusting the foundation you've laid and encouraging your teen to take ownership of their Jiu-Jitsu experience. This stage is as much about fostering their independence as it is about maintaining a connection that supports their growth.

GUIDING TEENS TOWARD
SELF-DRIVEN GROWTH

By the teenage years, motivation for Jiu-Jitsu needs to come from within. Younger kids might train because their parents encourage them, but teenagers thrive when their involvement aligns with their personal goals and interests.

As a parent, your role shifts from leading the charge to supporting from the sidelines. Encourage your teen to take ownership of their training journey. Whether their goal is to master specific techniques, prepare for a competition, or simply stay consistent, let them define what success looks like for themselves. This autonomy fosters responsibility and a deeper connection to the Art.

Practical Tip:

Keep the conversation open and collaborative. Ask questions like, "What are you most excited about improving right now?" or "How can I support you in staying on track with your goals?" These discussions empower your teen to reflect on their progress and involve you as a supportive partner in their journey.

HELPING THEM HANDLE
COMPETITIVE PRESSURE

For teenagers who compete, tournaments often take on greater significance. Matches are tougher, the stakes feel higher, and the fear of failure can weigh heavily. Your role as a parent is to help them navigate these pressures without amplifying them.

Encourage your teen to focus on effort and improvement rather than just results. Reinforce that their value isn't tied to the outcome of a match, but to their preparation, determination, and sportsmanship. Equip them with tools to manage stress and build confidence, reminding them that every competition—win or lose—is a step forward in their journey.

Practical Tips:

Reframe Nerves as Excitement: Help your teen see nerves as a sign that they care. Explain that these feelings are normal and can fuel their performance when channeled positively.

Introduce Mindfulness Techniques: Practice deep breathing, visualization, or grounding exercises together to help them stay centered. Encourage them to visualize success or focus on their strengths before stepping on the mat.

Encourage a Pre-Match Routine: Support them in developing habits like listening to music, stretching, or mentally rehearsing their game plan. A consistent routine fosters a sense of control and calm.

Foster Positive Self-Talk: Work with your teen to develop affirmations that replace doubts with empowering statements like, "I'm ready for this," "I did the work," or "I trust my skills." Practicing these regularly makes them second nature.

By focusing on effort and creating strategies for managing pressure, you're equipping your teen with the confidence to embrace competition as a positive, growth-filled experience.

THE PARENT-COACH RELATIONSHIP: WHEN TO STEP BACK

As teenagers grow, they become more capable of building direct and meaningful relationships with their coaches. This stage is an opportunity for them to take greater ownership of their training and trust their coach's guidance. Your role is to support this growth by stepping back just enough to let these connections strengthen.

Stepping back doesn't mean disengaging—it's about finding the right balance. Stay involved to show your encouragement and interest, but allow your teen to advocate for their own needs and goals. Trust that their coach has their best interests at heart, and encourage your teen to do the same.

Practical Tips:

Address Concerns Privately: If you have questions about your teen's progress or training, approach the coach respectfully and privately. Open, collaborative conversations ensure your concerns are addressed without undermining the coach's authority.

Model and Encourage Respect: Your attitude toward the coach shapes how your teen views them. Show confidence in their coach's expertise, and encourage your teen to communicate openly and respectfully.

Foster Independence: Support your teen in asking questions and seeking feedback directly from their coach. This builds their confidence in advocating for themselves.

By trusting the relationship between your teen and their coach, you're helping them build a bond of mutual respect and mentorship—one that can last a lifetime.

PREPARING FOR BIGGER OPPORTUNITIES

As your teen's skills grow, so might their opportunities—whether it's competing at a higher level, traveling for tournaments, or exploring scholarships and sponsorships. These experiences can be exciting and rewarding but may also bring new challenges. Your role is to support their ambitions while helping them stay grounded and balanced.

Encourage your teen to embrace growth as a lifelong process. Achievements like championships and sponsorships are wonderful milestones, but the real rewards lie in the discipline, resilience, and respect they develop along the way. Remind them that every step—win or lose—contributes to their growth as both an athlete and an individual.

Practical Tips:

Promote Balance: Encourage your teen to balance their Jiu-Jitsu aspirations with academics, social life, and downtime. Success in the sport should complement their overall development, not overshadow other important aspects of their life.

Celebrate Their Effort: Whether they win a medal or learn from a challenging match, highlight the effort they put in and the lessons they've gained.

Keep the Bigger Picture in Mind: Help your teen reflect on how Jiu-Jitsu contributes to their personal growth and future. Reinforce that the skills they're building extend far beyond the mat.

By supporting your teen's goals while emphasizing balance, you're helping them enjoy the journey and stay focused on what truly matters—becoming a strong, resilient, and well-rounded individual.

SUPPORTING RESPECT
AND GRATITUDE

Teenagers are at a stage where they can truly appreciate the deeper values of Jiu-Jitsu. Help them reflect on the importance of respect—respect for their coaches, teammates, opponents, and the art itself. Equally, encourage gratitude for the opportunities and challenges that shape their journey, as these experiences help them grow as both athletes and individuals.

Teach your teen to view every match and sparring session as a partnership. Opponents provide the challenges they need to improve, teammates motivate them to push harder, and coaches offer invaluable guidance. Gratitude for these connections fosters humility, strengthens relationships, and creates a positive training environment.

Practical Tips:

Model Respect: Show respect in your own interactions—with coaches, teammates, other parents, and opponents. A sincere thank-you to the coach after class or polite interactions at tournaments demonstrate the values of respect and humility.

Encourage Gratitude in Action: Prompt your teen to thank their coaches, training partners, and even their opponents after matches or training sessions. Acknowledging these relationships reinforces the values of mutual growth and collaboration.

Make Gratitude a Habit: At home, take moments to reflect together on what they're grateful for in their Jiu-Jitsu journey—whether it's a supportive coach, a new technique they've learned, or the camaraderie of teammates.

By fostering respect and gratitude, you're helping your teen embrace the values that make Jiu-Jitsu more than just a sport. These qualities will stay with them, shaping how they approach life itself.

PRACTICAL TIPS FOR PARENTS

Be a Listener: Teenagers crave independence but still value having someone who listens without judgment. Let them know you're there to hear their thoughts, concerns, and triumphs, offering guidance only when needed.

Support Without Hovering: Stay engaged by attending events or asking about their training, but give them the space to take charge of their journey. Allowing them to own their progress builds confidence and accountability.

Reinforce Balance: Help them establish a healthy routine that prioritizes school, social life, rest, and training. Demonstrate that balance is key to long-term success and overall well-being.

Encourage Humility: Emphasize the value of staying humble in victory and gracious in defeat. Celebrate their effort, sportsmanship, and growth over the outcome of a match.

CONCLUSION FOR THIS AGE GROUP

The teenage years are a transformative phase, marked by growth in every aspect of life—physically, mentally, and emotionally. By supporting your teen's independence, fostering open communication, and reinforcing values like respect and gratitude, you're equipping them with tools to succeed not just in Jiu-Jitsu, but in every area of life. Watching them mature into confident, compassionate, and capable individuals is one of the most rewarding parts of parenting.

"Success is no accident.

It is hard work,

perseverance,

learning, studying,

sacrifice,

and most of all,

love of what you are doing."

- Pelé

YOUR FEEDBACK MATTERS

Thank you for reading *The Jiu Jitsu Parents*. If you enjoy this book, I would be truly grateful if you could take a moment to leave a review on Amazon.

Your feedback not only helps others discover the book, but also supports my continued work as an author.

Scan the QR code below to go directly to the review page:

or visit:
https://www.amazon.com/review/create-review?asin=B0DWDM44H9

With appreciation Philippe Eggert

Part B:
General Principles of
Being a Supportive Parent.

INTRODUCTION

As parents, our love for our children often pushes us to want the best for them—to help them avoid the mistakes we made, seize opportunities we missed, and reach their fullest potential. But in our eagerness to guide and protect, it's easy to overlook one of the most important aspects of parenting: being truly supportive.

Encouragement doesn't mean stepping in to take over their path or projecting our dreams onto them. It means walking alongside them, trusting their instincts, and giving them space to make their own choices—even if that includes stumbling and learning from their mistakes.

I've fallen into the "but I know what's best for you" mindset more times than I'd like to admit. It's natural to believe that our experiences give us the insight to steer them in the right direction. But what we often forget is that our children aren't extensions of us. They have their own dreams, personalities, and timelines, and it's our job to honor that.

This section is about recalibrating our approach as parents. It's a reminder that being supportive isn't about controlling the outcome but about creating an environment where our children feel safe to explore their passions and challenges on their own terms.

In the sections ahead, we'll explore practical strategies to foster this kind of environment— whether it's at home, in the gym, or through your relationship with your child. You'll learn how to balance motivation with patience, guide them through setbacks, and embrace the deeper life lessons this process offers.

Because at the end of the day, our role isn't to dictate their journey but to celebrate the unique individuals they're becoming.

5. CREATING A POSITIVE ENVIRONMENT AT HOME

Jiu-Jitsu is a way of life that becomes part of your child's identity. Like any lifestyle, it thrives when supported by a strong and nurturing foundation at home. As a parent, your role goes beyond getting them to practice or cheering at tournaments. It's about creating a space where they feel understood and encouraged—where effort is valued, mistakes are part of learning, and they have room to grow.

The routines, habits, and attitudes you foster at home shape how your child approaches the challenges they face, helping them build a mindset that supports their growth. This positive environment is the soil where their roots take hold, giving them all they need to flourish in their own unique way.

ENCOURAGING HEALTHY ROUTINES

Jiu-Jitsu can be demanding, and healthy routines at home make a big difference. Sleep, nutrition, and recovery don't just support their training—they help your child feel energized, focused, and ready for whatever comes next.

Practical Tips:

Prioritize Sleep: Establish a bedtime routine that works for your child's age and needs. For younger kids, an 8:00 PM bedtime with 10–15 minutes of reading together can help them unwind. As they grow, adjust the timing slightly but keep the routine consistent. Make it clear that staying up late doesn't benefit anyone—after all, the early bird catches the worm. Talk to them about how sleep helps their body recover, their muscles grow, and their mind reset for the next day.

Fuel Their Growth: Meals don't need to be complicated, but balance is key. Provide real food: fruits, vegetables, good fats, and proteins. Involve your child in meal planning and cooking whenever possible, so they also learn important life skills. Limit processed snacks and make sugary drinks a no-go!

Water is life and the best choice for your kids—it must be the go-to beverage. Get them a cool refill bottle they love to make drinking water fun and easy.

Make Recovery Non-Negotiable: Teach your child that recovery is just as important as hard training. Rest days are essential for staying healthy and making progress. Support their recovery with science-backed practices like proper hydration, quality sleep, and nutrient-rich meals. After intense sessions, encourage effective habits like gentle stretching, foam rolling, or even ice baths to reduce inflammation. If you have access, a sauna can be a great way to relax muscles and promote circulation.

TEACHING EMOTIONAL REGULATION AND RESILIENCE

Jiu-Jitsu challenges your child in ways that go far beyond physical technique. They'll face setbacks, tough losses, moments of self-doubt and frustrations. Teaching them emotional regulation and resilience at home gives them the tools to approach these challenges with a positive and healthy mindset.

Practical Tips:

Model Calmness: Children often mirror what they see. When things don't go as planned, demonstrate calm and thoughtful responses. For example, "I felt frustrated earlier, but I took a moment to breathe and figure out the next step."

Talk About Setbacks: Help your child see setbacks as opportunities to learn. If they're upset after a tough moment, ask, "What do you think we could do differently next time?" Share a personal story about a time when persistence helped you overcome a challenge.

Practice Problem-Solving: Encourage your child to think through their challenges instead of solving them for them. Ask, "What's one small step we could take to make this better?" This builds independence and critical thinking skills they'll carry with them.

MODELING POSITIVE BEHAVIOR

Children absorb the actions, attitudes, and habits they see at home. The way you respond to challenges, communicate with others, and approach daily tasks creates a powerful example for your child. Modeling positive behavior at home sets the tone for how they approach their own challenges, relationships, and responsibilities.

Practical Tips:

Show Patience in Tough Moments: When things get frustrating, whether it's a late dinner or a misplaced item, demonstrate patience and calm. For example, say, "I'm frustrated, but let's figure this out together," instead of reacting with anger.

Communicate Respectfully: Speak to family members and others with kindness, even in disagreements. Your tone and words show your child how to handle conflict without negativity.

Celebrate Effort Over Perfection: Praise your child's effort in chores or schoolwork, rather than focusing solely on results. For instance, "I'm proud of how much thought you put into this," helps your child feel recognized for their process, not just their outcomes.

PRACTICAL TIPS FOR PARENTS

Create a Routine Together: Collaborate with your child to plan their weekly schedule, balancing Jiu-Jitsu, school, and downtime. This not only empowers them but also instills valuable time management skills.

Encourage Open Communication: Create a space where your child feels comfortable sharing their thoughts, frustrations, and achievements. Ask thoughtful questions about their day, like, "What's something that challenged you today, and how did you handle it?" or, "Did anything make you feel proud or excited today?" or, "What's something you wish had gone differently, and why?" These questions invite deeper conversations and help your child feel truly understood.

Celebrate Effort: Instead of focusing on outcomes, highlight specific actions or choices your child made. "I saw how much thought you put into solving that problem," or, "You didn't give up even when it got tricky." Recognizing these moments helps your child understand that their effort matters.

Be Consistently Present: Being present isn't about grand gestures—it's about showing up consistently in your child's everyday life. Whether it's helping them prepare for the next day or sharing quiet moments together, your steady presence helps them feel secure and valued.

CONCLUSION FOR THE SECTION

A positive home environment isn't built in a day—it's created through small actions—an ongoing process. The way you listen, support, and model behavior becomes the foundation your child relies on as they grow. By staying engaged, celebrating their effort, and being consistently present, you show them they are valued and supported. This sense of support extends beyond their Jiu-Jitsu journey and into every part of their life.

"The way we talk

to our children

becomes

their inner voice."

- Peggy O'Mara

6. THE PARENT-COACH PARTNERSHIP

Handing over the reins isn't easy at all—especially when it comes to your child. Coaches often become the voice your child listens to most closely, influencing not just their skill development, but also their personality and progress. It's a strange mix of emotions we experience—pride, hesitation, and the urge to step in when things feel unfamiliar.

This partnership is about trust. Your child needs to feel your support, while also having the space to build their own connection with their coach. By respecting the coach's role and trusting their approach, you're helping to create an environment where your child feels guided and supported from all sides.

In this section, we'll explore how to build a productive relationship with the coach—one rooted in mutual respect and trust. Together, you'll create a dynamic that supports your child's growth and fosters a positive training experience.

BUILDING TRUST AND RESPECT
WITH COACHES

Trust is the essence of a successful parent-coach partnership. It begins with respecting the coach's expertise and understanding that their methods, even if different from your expectations, are intended to guarantee your child's success. Each coach has a unique style—some might be firm, others more laid-back—but what matters most is their dedication to steer your child's progress and development.

As a parent, it's natural to feel protective or even uncertain about how your child is being guided. By stepping back and trusting the coach's approach, you reinforce the value of respect and teamwork while allowing your child to develop a healthy, independent relationship with their coach.

Practical Tips:

Communicate Clearly: Share your child's goals, strengths, or areas they're struggling with early on. For instance, if they've mentioned feeling unsure about certain techniques or situations, letting the coach know allows them to provide support tailored to your child's needs.

Respect Boundaries: Let the coach lead during training sessions and avoid stepping in or questioning their methods, especially in front of your child. If you have concerns, discuss them privately and respectfully to maintain trust.

Show Appreciation: A simple "thank you, coach" after class or a note of gratitude for their efforts can go a long way in building mutual respect and a positive dynamic.

KNOWING WHEN TO INTERVENE
AND WHEN TO STEP BACK

Navigating the balance between stepping in and stepping back can be one of the trickiest parts of building a strong parent-coach relationship. As parents, it's natural to feel protective, thinking we know what's best, when something doesn't sit right —whether it's a concern about your child's progress or how they're being coached. But part of fostering a productive dynamic is knowing when to trust the coach to handle things and when it's appropriate to raise a concern.

If you notice your child is struggling with a challenge in training, resist the urge to intervene right away. Allowing the coach to address these moments demonstrates trust and reinforces their role as a guide. However, if you observe issues that go beyond the scope of training—such as signs of disrespect, safety concerns, or behavior that negatively impacts your child—it's important to speak with the coach privately and constructively. This ensures open communication without undermining their authority.

Practical Tips:

Step Back During Training: Resist the urge to jump in with advice during practice. Let the coach lead instruction and corrections. This not only helps your child learn to trust their coach but also reinforces their ability to take direction and grow through the process.

Intervene When Necessary: If you notice a serious issue, such as safety concerns, bullying, or unprofessional behavior, address it promptly. Approach the conversation with the coach calmly and constructively, focusing on collaboration to find a solution that ensures your child's well-being.

Encourage Independence: Support your child in speaking up for themselves. For instance, if they're struggling with a technique, suggest they ask their coach for help rather than stepping in on their behalf. This builds their confidence and teaches them to take responsibility for their learning.

SUPPORTING THE TEAM CULTURE

Jiu-Jitsu may seem like an individual sport, but it thrives on teamwork and collaboration. Coaches, teammates, and training partners play a vital role in your child's development. By embracing and supporting the team culture, you help foster a positive and encouraging environment that benefits everyone involved.

Practical Tips:

Be a Role Model: Demonstrate respect for coaches, teammates, and fellow parents through your actions. Whether it's how you handle conversations, observe classes, or cheer at tournaments, your example reinforces the values of respect and teamwork that define the Jiu-Jitsu community.

Encourage Team Spirit: Actively celebrate the successes of your child's teammates, showing them that every achievement contributes to the team's growth. Highlight how learning from one another's strengths builds a supportive and collaborative environment for everyone.

Avoid Sideline Coaching: Trust the coach's expertise during training and competitions, allowing them to guide your child without conflicting messages. By maintaining a calm and encouraging presence on the sidelines, you help reinforce your child's focus and respect for the coaching process.

PRACTICAL TIPS FOR PARENTS

Be Open to Feedback: When coaches offer constructive input about your child's progress, view it as valuable guidance for their development. Approach feedback with an open mind, recognizing it as a shared effort to help your child succeed.

Communicate Regularly: Keep regular communication with the coach to stay informed, but be mindful of their time and responsibilities. Focus on building a collaborative relationship by addressing questions or concerns respectfully and constructively.

Focus on the Big Picture: Remember that a coach's role goes beyond teaching techniques—they're guiding your child's development as both an athlete and an individual. Support their expertise and the collaborative journey they create to help your child thrive.

CONCLUSION FOR THE SECTION

Supporting the team culture is about creating a space where everyone—parents, coaches, and teammates—can thrive together. By showing respect, fostering trust, and encouraging collaboration, you help strengthen the bonds that make the Jiu-Jitsu journey so much more rewarding for your child and the entire community.

"Trust is the glue of life.

It's the most essential

ingredient in effective

communication.

It's the foundational

principle that holds

all relationships."

- Stephen R. Covey

7. ENCOURAGING
WITHOUT PRESSURING

There are not many things as rewarding and wonderful as watching our children succeed. It's so easy, though, to get caught up in the spiral of wanting them to achieve more and not realizing how our actions—though coming from a pure heart and the best intentions—can sometimes create pressure we don't even realize. In our drive to help them, we can lose sight of their perspective, unintentionally making their experience feel more like an obligation —a chore—than something they can truly enjoy.

Encouraging without pressuring is a delicate balancing act. It's about understanding how to offer support that uplifts rather than overwhelms, and recognizing when to trust their process instead of trying to steer it. By focusing on their growth, not outcomes, we create a space where they feel confident to explore their own potential while holding onto the joy that makes Jiu-Jitsu truly special.

RECOGNIZING THE SIGNS OF PRESSURE

Even the most well-intentioned encouragement can sometimes feel like pressure to a child. This often shows up in subtle ways—your child might start dreading training sessions, withdrawing from teammates, or focusing too much on trying to please you. They may express anxiety about not meeting expectations or suddenly lose the spark they once had for Jiu-Jitsu.

As parents, it's easy to miss these signs in the moment. We're so focused on their success and improvements that we don't always realize how our words or actions might weigh on them. A packed schedule, a well-meaning comment, or even quiet expectations can turn something they love into something that feels more like a burden. These moments aren't failures—they're opportunities to pause and reconnect with what truly matters.

Pressure isn't always obvious. It can build gradually, fueled by small, unnoticed actions or misplaced focus on constant progress. By staying sensitive to changes in their energy and enthusiasm, we can adjust our approach and help them feel supported in their journey. This allows them to reconnect with the joy and excitement that make Jiu-Jitsu such a special part of their lives.

Practical Tips:

Notice the Small Changes: Watch for subtle shifts in their behavior, like reluctance to go to training, quiet moments after class, or being unusually hard on themselves. These small signs can indicate that something is off.

Ask Open-Ended Questions: Instead of performance-focused questions like, "How did you do today?" try asking, "How are you feeling about training right now?" This opens the opportunity for them to share what's on their mind.

Reflect on Your Actions: Take a step back and think about how your words or actions might affect them. Are you focusing too much on results or unintentionally making them feel they need to meet certain expectations?

Balance Healthy Pressure: A little challenge can motivate, but too much pressure can weigh them down. Pay attention to how they respond and adjust your approach to help them feel supported. It's not about being "soft" on them—it's about finding the right balance to push them out of their comfort zones without taking away the joy.

SHIFTING THE FOCUS
TO EFFORT AND GROWTH

It's easy to celebrate and focus on the achievements and milestones—the medals, the stripes, the belts. But if we're not careful, we might unintentionally teach our kids that these are the only things that matter. The constant push to achieve can make them feel like their worth is tied to results. For a child, that kind of focus can feel like quiet pressure, turning their hard work into something measured by outcomes rather than progress.

Shifting the focus to effort means looking deeper. It's noticing the moments where they push through frustration to try again, the grit it takes to work on a technique that's giving them trouble, or the courage they show when stepping onto the mat. These are the real victories—ones that don't come with trophies but shape who they are.

When we celebrate their hard work, we show them that success isn't about being the best. It's about becoming better and embracing the process. Over time, this mindset builds a love for the journey itself, where challenges become opportunities and growth becomes its own reward. These lessons will carry them far beyond the mats, helping them face life with the same determination and joy they've found in Jiu-Jitsu.

Practical Tips:

Praise Their Hard Work: Instead of emphasizing the result, highlight their effort. Say things like, "You've been working so hard on that sweep—it's really paying off," or, "I'm so proud of how focused you've been during sparring."

Celebrate Small Wins: Recognize moments that might go unnoticed, like overcoming frustration with a challenging technique or showing courage in a tough match. These small victories build confidence and reinforce the value of persistence.

Reframe Setbacks as Growth: When they struggle or fall short, remind them that every step forward— even the tough ones—contributes to their progress. Share phrases like, "Every challenge you face makes you stronger," to reinforce the idea that effort is part of the journey.

LETTING THEM TAKE THE LEAD

As your child matures, there comes a time when stepping back allows them to step forward. When they feel trusted to make choices about their training, they develop a stronger sense of ownership and motivation. By giving them this trust, we offer them the opportunity to connect more deeply with the art —not because they're following instructions, but because they're finding their own reasons to stay committed.

Letting them take the lead doesn't mean stepping away entirely. It's about recognizing those moments when they're ready to decide for themselves— whether it's choosing which techniques to focus on, deciding how to approach a tough class, or even deciding when to rest. Some decisions will work out great, and some not so much, but that's the process of learning. These choices not only build their independence but also show them that their voice matters in shaping their journey.

For parents, this can be one of the hardest parts of the process. The instinct to step in, to guide, or to protect doesn't just go away. But sometimes, the most meaningful support is simply standing beside them, ready to cheer them on when they succeed or offer perspective when things don't go as planned. By giving them this space, you're not stepping back —you're helping them step forward on their own path toward strength, confidence, and a lifelong love for Jiu-Jitsu.

Practical Tips:

Ask for Their Input: Encourage open conversations by asking questions like, "What would you like to focus on this week?" or "Is there something you feel excited to work on during sparring?" These questions give them the space to express their preferences and take ownership of their decisions.

Respect Their Choices: Listen without judgment when they share their decisions or reasoning. Acknowledge their perspective with phrases like, "I see why that's important to you," or, "That sounds like a great plan—I trust your decision." This helps build their confidence and sense of independence.

Step Back Without Disengaging: Give them time to make decisions, even if some might not work out as expected. For example, let them choose what competition they want to sign up for or what they want to focus on in sparring. Be present to guide them if needed, but allow them to experience the learning process on their terms.

AVOIDING COMPARISONS

In Jiu-Jitsu, progress is as individual as the kids on the mats. Some pick up techniques quickly, some are fast, some are strong, some have a natural talent, and some bring an uplifting personality. It's easy to look around and notice differences—how one teammate seems to master moves effortlessly or how another is already competing at a higher level. But each one is on their own journey, moving at their own pace. Comparing your child to others, even with the best intentions, can unintentionally chip away at their confidence and enthusiasm.

Every child's journey is their own, shaped by their unique talents, strengths, and challenges. When we let go of comparisons, we give them the space to focus on what really matters: their personal growth and love for the art. By celebrating the effort they put in and the progress they make—no matter how big or small—we help them see that their value lies in who they are, not in how they perform compared to others.

Our role is to remind them that growth isn't a race and that success doesn't have to look the same for everyone. Whether they're mastering a new technique or simply showing up with a positive attitude, every step forward is worth celebrating.

Practical Tips:

Focus on Their Unique Journey: Help your child see their progress as their own. Highlight moments that reflect their growth, like, "You've been working so hard, and it's great to see how far you've come," or, "It's wonderful how you're becoming more comfortable and confident on the mat."

Celebrate Individual Strengths: Take time to recognize what makes your child special. Whether it's their persistence, creativity, or ability to support teammates, acknowledging these qualities helps build their self-esteem and appreciation for their unique abilities.

Model Positive Behavior: Avoid making comparisons yourself, even casually, by refraining from comments like, "Try doing it next time like Kris..." Instead, set the example by celebrating your child's individuality and appreciating the diversity of their teammates' skills and strengths.

PRACTICAL TIPS FOR PARENTS

Be a Cheerleader, Not a Coach: Focus on supporting your child's enthusiasm and effort rather than critiquing techniques. For instance, cheer them on by saying, "I'm so proud of how focused you were today," instead of offering corrections. Your role is to celebrate their journey, not to step into the coach's role.

Celebrate Milestones, Big and Small: From earning a stripe to showing kindness to a teammate, recognize both big and small moments that highlight their progress. For example, "I saw how you helped your teammate during drills—that was awesome teamwork!" These moments reinforce their confidence and joy in Jiu-Jitsu.

Stay Patient and Positive: Progress isn't always linear, and some days will be tougher than others. Remind your child that growth takes time and encourage them by saying, "It's okay if today felt hard—it's all part of getting better." This teaches them that perseverance is more important than perfection.

CONCLUSION FOR THE SECTION

Encouraging without pressuring means finding the balance between being a steady source of support and allowing your child the freedom to discover their own path. By focusing on their progress, celebrating their strengths, and letting them take ownership of their journey, you're showing them that their worth isn't tied to results or comparisons, but to the courage and effort they bring to every challenge.

These lessons will stay with them far beyond the mats. When children feel seen, valued, and trusted, they develop the confidence to embrace who they are and the resilience to face life's challenges on their own terms. You're not just helping them grow in Jiu-Jitsu—you're empowering them to thrive in every part of their life.

"Encouragement

is a gentle hand,

not a firm grip.

It points the way

but lets the traveler walk."

- Zen teaching

8. HANDLING SETBACKS
AND INJURIES

Every Jiu-Jitsu journey comes with its fair share of challenges—whether it's struggling with a new technique, losing a hard-fought match, or recovering from an injury. These moments can feel overwhelming, especially for a child, but they also hold some of the most valuable lessons. How we, as parents, respond to these setbacks and difficulties plays a key role in shaping how our children experience and overcome adversity.

Watching your child struggle isn't easy—it's heartbreaking. There's a natural instinct to step in and fix the problem, or to shield them from discomfort at all costs. But growth often comes from these very struggles. It's about helping them see that setbacks aren't roadblocks—they're stepping stones toward becoming stronger and more confident. By guiding them to process these moments with patience and perspective, you're giving them the tools to face challenges with courage and resilience.

It's not about taking away the hard moments—it's about being there with them as they navigate the ups and downs. These challenges, when met with steady support, can become defining moments in their journey, building the foundation for their confidence and love for Jiu-Jitsu.

SUPPORTING RECOVERY AND REHABILITATION

Injuries are an inevitable part of any physical activity, and Jiu-Jitsu is no exception. For a child, being injured often means facing uncomfortable limitations —whether it's losing the ability to train, struggling with everyday movements, or feeling left out of their gym community. These challenges can be just as emotionally draining as they are physically difficult.

As parents, this is your opportunity to offer steady, thoughtful support. Encourage your child to focus on what they can do—whether it's small milestones in their recovery exercises, joining their teammates to observe class, or finding ways to stay involved without physical strain. Celebrate the progress they make, no matter how incremental, and remind them that recovery is a step forward, not something holding them back.

Impatience, frustration, sadness, or even anger might surface during the times of rehabilitation, and your presence matters most in those moments. By being there to listen and offer reassurance, you're helping them stay connected to their passion while building confidence in their ability to recover and return stronger.

Practical Tips:

Focus on What They Can Do: Help your child stay engaged by shifting the focus to small, achievable goals. Whether it's practicing light movements approved by their doctor, observing their teammates in class, or visualizing techniques, remind them that progress happens in many forms. Add a playful twist by turning exercises into mini-challenges, like counting how many perfect reps they can do or timing their recovery stretches.

Create a Routine for Recovery: Work with your child to establish a simple, consistent recovery plan. Setting times for exercises, rest, and even attending class to observe can help them feel a sense of structure and control during this phase. Incorporate something fun, like using their favorite music during rehab sessions or setting a "goal reward" for milestones they reach.

Acknowledge Their Emotions: Rehabilitation can bring up feelings of impatience, sadness, or frustration. Be there to listen without judgment. Saying something like, "It's okay to feel this way—it shows how much you care," can help them feel seen and supported. Balance these moments with opportunities for lighthearted connection, like watching funny videos or talking about what they're excited to do when they're back on the mat.

Celebrate Small Wins Together: Recovery is a journey, and every step forward matters. Cheer for progress like regaining a movement or completing a set of exercises. Highlight their effort with encouragement like, "That's a big step—you're doing great!" Make celebrating fun by creating little "recovery trophies" or rewards for milestones, like a favorite meal or activity.

Stay Patient and Positive: Recovery takes time, and slower progress may happen along the way. Show your child that you're in this together by modeling patience and keeping the atmosphere positive. Lighten the mood with playful activities that fit their abilities, like inventing a recovery game or coming up with funny nicknames for their exercises.

TEACHING THE VALUE OF PATIENCE

Patience doesn't come naturally to most children—especially in Jiu-Jitsu, where progress can sometimes feel slow, and challenges can seem insurmountable. For kids who are eager to improve, being stuck on a technique or facing repeated difficulties can quickly turn into frustration. These moments, though difficult, are opportunities to help them see the bigger picture.

As parents, our role isn't to fix their frustration but to guide them toward understanding that growth takes time. Patience isn't just about waiting—it's about staying engaged, finding value in the small steps, and trusting the process. By helping them focus on their progress and effort rather than immediate results, you're teaching them that every challenge has its place in the journey.

Practical Tips:

Celebrate the Small Steps: Point out and praise your child's progress, even in the smallest areas. Acknowledge their efforts by saying things like, "It's amazing how much progress you've made with this technique," or, "You're showing such great focus and persistence."

Model Patience Yourself: Show your child how you practice patience in your own life. For instance, share moments when you've had to wait for something important or when you've taken time to achieve a goal. Leading by example helps them see patience in action.

Create Opportunities to Practice: Introduce fun activities that naturally build patience, like puzzles, games that require strategy, or even mindful breathing exercises. These can be simple ways to help them develop focus and self-control while having fun.

Reframe Waiting as Positive: Instead of letting waiting or slow progress feel frustrating, reframe it as part of the process. For example, say, "Learning something well takes time—just like building strength or improving a technique," to help them embrace the journey.

Encourage Reflection: After a challenging practice or competition, ask your child what they learned about themselves. Questions like, "What was the hardest part for you today?" or, "What are you most proud of sticking with?" can help them see how patience contributes to growth.

HELPING THEM NAVIGATE LOSSES

Losing a match is never easy, especially for kids who are still learning how to process disappointment. For them, each loss can feel magnified—like a reflection of their worth or effort. As parents, it's natural to feel the sting of their emotions, but these moments are also powerful opportunities to guide them toward growth.

Your role in these moments isn't to fix the pain or brush it aside but to help them see losses as part of the process. They're not a measure of failure— they're stepping stones for learning. By staying calm, encouraging reflection, and celebrating their courage, you can help them take valuable lessons from defeat while keeping their love for Jiu-Jitsu alive.

Practical Tips:

Normalize Losing: Remind your child that every athlete, even the greatest champions, experiences defeat. Use examples of role models in the sport who've learned and grown through losses. Frame losing as a normal, necessary part of improvement.

Focus on What They Gained: Instead of emphasizing what went wrong, shift the focus to what they gained. Ask, "What's one thing you're proud of from that match?" or "What do you want to work on next?" This helps reframe the experience in a positive light.

Celebrate Their Courage: Stepping onto the mat takes bravery, regardless of the outcome. Let them know how much you admire their determination and effort, saying things like, "It was amazing to see you give it your all out there," or "I loved how you didn't give up, even when it got tough."

Give Them Space to Feel: Losses can be emotional, and that's okay. Let your child express frustration or sadness without rushing to fix it. Simply saying, "I'm here if you want to talk about it," shows them that their feelings are valid and supported.

Create a Small Ritual for Reflection: After a match, use a simple routine to reflect on the day. For example, talk about one thing they enjoyed, one thing they learned, and one thing they'd like to work on. This builds a habit of growth-focused thinking.

Building a growth mindset in your child means helping them see challenges not as barriers, but as opportunities to learn and grow. It's about shifting the focus from instant success to steady progress, and from fear of failure to curiosity about what's possible. In Jiu-Jitsu, this can mean embracing the lessons from a tough roll, sticking with a challenging technique, or finding pride in their effort even when results aren't immediate.

As parents, your encouragement plays a pivotal role. By focusing on their effort and progress rather than outcomes, you show them that improvement is a journey, not a destination. This mindset doesn't just help them on the mats—it equips them with the resilience and adaptability they'll carry through every challenge they face in life.

Practical Tips:

Praise the Process, Not Just Results: Highlight their hard work and persistence instead of focusing on outcomes. Say things like, "I'm so proud of how much effort you put into learning that technique," rather than, "You're so good at this."

Encourage Questions and Curiosity: Create a safe space for your child to ask questions about techniques or challenges they face. Phrases like, "What part do you think was the trickiest today?" or, "What's something you'd like to try differently next time?" can spark curiosity and exploration.

Model Growth Mindset Thinking: Share moments from your own life when you faced setbacks and used them to improve. For example, "I wasn't great at presentations at first, but I kept practicing and eventually got more comfortable."

Celebrate Failures as Opportunities: When things don't go their way, reframe the experience. Say, "This is how we learn and get better—every mistake shows us something important," to help them embrace challenges.

Use "Yet" to Reframe Struggles: When your child says, "I can't do this," encourage them to add "yet." For example, "I can't do this yet, but I'm working on it," helps shift their focus from inability to progress.

PRACTICAL TIPS FOR PARENTS

Encourage Patience and Perspective: Remind your child that progress isn't always immediate. Use phrases like, "Every small step you take brings you closer to where you want to be," to help them focus on the journey rather than the outcome.

Support Their Emotional Well-Being: Acknowledge their feelings of frustration, sadness, or impatience, and create space for them to express these emotions. Phrases like, "I see how hard this is for you, and I'm here to support you," show that you're a steady presence during tough times.

Celebrate Incremental Progress: Recovery and growth come in small steps. Cheer for milestones, no matter how small, with genuine excitement. For example, "You worked hard on that today—your effort really shows!" reinforces their perseverance.

Stay Engaged Without Overstepping: Attend classes with them during recovery or watch together when they can't participate. Show interest in their observations about teammates or techniques to help them feel connected even when they're limited physically.

Model Patience and Resilience: Share examples from your own life of overcoming obstacles with time and effort. This shows them that setbacks are temporary and that persistence pays off.

Keep the Process Playful: Find creative ways to make recovery and growth fun. For instance, turn stretches or light exercises into games, or let them choose a reward for completing a part of their rehab routine.

CONCLUSION FOR THE SECTION

Every challenge your child faces in their Jiu-Jitsu journey—whether it's a tough loss, a stalled technique, or time away from training due to an injury —holds the potential to shape their character in meaningful ways. These moments may feel heavy at first, but they are the stepping stones to evolve. As a parents, our role in these times is not to fix or smooth over every bump in the road but to walk alongside our child, offering steady support and perspective. It's in these moments that they learn the true value of patience, the courage to face adversity, and the strength to rise again. Recovery, like growth, isn't always linear. Some days will be harder than others— full of frustration, restlessness, or even doubt. But with our guidance, our kids will come to see that setbacks aren't failures, they're part of the process. Every step forward, no matter how small, is a victory worth celebrating. What makes this journey meaningful is the bond you build through it—the conversations after a challenging match, the laughter during a "recovery game," and the quiet moments when your encouragement helps them believe in their own strength. These are the memories that will stay with them forever. So, when the hard days come —and they will—remember that your presence and belief in your child are the greatest gifts you can give them. Together, you'll turn difficulties into lessons, challenges into opportunities, and every injury into a story of resilience. Through it all, your child will grow

—not just as a Jiu-Jitsu athlete but as a strong, compassionate individual ready to take on the world.

"Strength doesn't come

from what you can do.

It comes from overcoming

the things you once thought

you couldn't."

- Rikki Rogers

9. LESSONS BEYOND THE MAT

Jiu-Jitsu, translated from Japanese as "the gentle art," offers far more than just techniques or principles —it's a practice that transforms how we navigate life in general. It teaches lessons in resilience, problem-solving, discipline, and respect that not only apply on the mats but ripple into every aspect of our children's lives.

You'll see these mindsets in action—when they tackle a tough math problem, support a friend through a hard time, or handle difficulties with quiet strength. What starts in a sparring session—figuring out how to escape a tricky position—becomes a way of thinking, a belief that there's always a way forward, no matter the challenge.

As parents, we have the privilege of walking alongside them in this journey. We see their growth, day by day—the courage it takes to step onto the mat, the humility they show when learning from a teammate, and the joy they find in mastering something they once thought impossible. And along the way, we grow too. Watching our children navigate struggles with determination and optimism inspires us to approach our own challenges in the same way, making their journey a mirror for our own growth.

So, celebrate these moments. Every roll, every win, every loss, and every lesson—they all add up to something far greater than competition or technique. They build the kind of character that will guide your child through life with strength, compassion, and confidence. And as you support them, remember: you're not just raising a Jiu-Jitsu athlete—you're raising a remarkable human being.

DISCIPLINE AND ACCOUNTABILITY

Jiu-Jitsu teaches kids that progress doesn't happen by accident—it's built through consistent effort and taking ownership of their actions. From showing up to class on time to practicing techniques with focus, these small habits shape their understanding of discipline. They begin to see that commitment isn't about perfection but about making a sincere effort, even when things get tough.

Accountability is a natural part of this journey. On the mats, kids learn that mistakes aren't something to avoid—they're opportunities to improve. Forgetting a step in a technique or skipping a training session teaches them to reflect on what went wrong and how they can do better. Over time, they develop the confidence to own their choices and the determination to keep moving forward.

For parents, supporting these values means creating an environment where kids can take responsibility. If they forget their gear or struggle with time management, it's a chance to guide them toward finding a solution rather than fixing it for them. At the same time, celebrating their effort—whether it's showing up on a hard day or learning from a mistake —reinforces the value of their actions.

Practical Tips:

Apply Lessons: Help your child see the connection between discipline in Jiu-Jitsu and daily life. For example, "The focus you use during drills is the same effort that helps with finishing your schoolwork."

Celebrate Responsibility: When your child follows through on commitments, like helping with chores or keeping a promise, acknowledge their effort. For instance, "That shows great accountability—just like in Jiu-Jitsu when you take responsibility for your training.

Encourage Ownership: If they forget to complete a task or make an error, guide them toward reflection without judgment. Say, "What could you do differently next time?" Connect it to Jiu-Jitsu by reminding them how they adjust techniques after sparring.

Model Accountability: Share real examples from your own life. For instance, "I didn't manage my time well today, but I reorganized my priorities to get back on track. It's important to own up to our responsibilities.

PROBLEM-SOLVING AND ADAPTABILITY

Jiu-Jitsu challenges our kids to think fast and adapt to new situations all the time. Whether they're solving the puzzle of escaping a tight submission or adjusting their approach mid-roll, every training session builds their ability to face uncertainty with confidence. Over time, these lessons transcend the mats, influencing how they tackle problems at school, at home, or in their social life.

What makes these lessons so powerful is their practicality. Problem-solving in Jiu-Jitsu isn't theoretical—it's hands-on. Your child learns to assess what's working, try new angles, and keep their composure when things don't go as planned. This adaptability becomes an anchor they can rely on when faced with challenges in other areas of life.

As parents, we can deepen this learning by drawing connections between their experiences in training and the hurdles they encounter in daily life.A tough sparring match can be a metaphor for managing a challenging assignment or navigating a disagreement with a friend. By reinforcing these connections, you help your child internalize the mindset that every challenge is -- An opportunity to grow.

Practical Tips:

Draw Real-Life Parallels: When your child encounters challenges outside of training, remind them of a similar experience from Jiu-Jitsu. For example, "Remember how you stayed calm and tried different grips to pass the guard? What's a way you can adapt your approach here?"

Encourage Small Adjustments: Reinforce the value of iteration by focusing on progress over perfection. After a tough experience, ask, "What's one small thing you could do differently next time?" This builds confidence in their ability to adapt and improve.

Celebrate Creative Thinking: Highlight moments when your child finds unique solutions, whether on the mat or at home. For example, "I saw how you solved that issue with your teammate during practice —that's the kind of thinking that helps in every part of life.

RESILIENCE AND GRIT

Jiu-Jitsu is a journey filled with challenges, from mastering complex techniques to overcoming tough losses. It teaches our kids that resilience isn't about avoiding failure—it's about finding the strength to keep going, even when it's hard. Each stumble on the mat becomes a stepping stone to building their grit.

In the face of setbacks, it teaches our kids the value of perseverance. They learn that progress is built through consistent effort and determination. Over time, these lessons shape how they tackle difficulties, whether it's in school, friendships, or personal goals.

As parents, we can nurture this growth by helping our children recognize the value of persistence and effort. It's not about shielding them from tough moments but guiding them through with encouragement and the perspective that setbacks are part of the process.

Practical Tips:

Notice Small Victories: Celebrate when your child sticks with something challenging, like finishing a school project or solving a difficult task. For example, you might tell them, "You worked so hard on this, and look at what you accomplished. That's real grit in action—great job!"

Model Perseverance: Share moments when you faced challenges and stayed determined. For example, "I didn't think I could finish that work project, but I kept going step by step, and it felt so good when I finally completed it."

Encourage Consistent Effort: Remind your child that resilience grows through regular effort. Let them know, "It's not about being perfect—it's about keep going and giving it your best shot."

RESPECT AND GRATITUDE

In Jiu-Jitsu, respect is woven into every interaction. It begins with the small gestures—a bow when stepping onto the mat, a fist bump before sparring, or a handshake after a challenging roll. Over time, these actions evolve into something deeper: a recognition of the people who guide, push, and inspire your child. Respect means valuing their coach for their mentorship, their teammates for their camaraderie, and even their opponents for the lessons they provide.

Gratitude builds on this foundation. It's the thank-you to a coach who patiently shares their knowledge, or the appreciation for a training partner who challenges them during a tough session. These consistent acts of acknowledgment teach your child to see their progress as a collective effort—not just their own, but one shaped by the support of others.

As parents, our role is to bring these values to life. Respect isn't just what we tell our kids to practice— it's how we treat their coach, support their teammates, and handle frustrations at tournaments. Gratitude isn't about reminding them to say "thank you"—it's about showing them how to recognize and honor the contributions of others. By living these values, we give our children the tools to carry respect and gratitude into every interaction they have.

Practical Tips:

Acts of Respect: Encourage your child to take simple, intentional steps to show respect, such as offering help to a teammate who seems overwhelmed, giving a genuine compliment after a tough match, or contributing to post-class cleanup. These practical actions reinforce respect in ways that are easy to integrate into their routine.

Moments That Mattered: After an event or class, ask your child to reflect on when they felt most supported or when they offered support to someone else. For instance, "Did you notice how your partner appreciated your encouragement during drills?" or "How did it feel when your coach praised your focus today?" These discussions make respect and gratitude relatable and impactful.

Lead by Example: Let your child see respect and gratitude in action through your behavior. Thank their coach personally for their insights, or express admiration for a teammate's perseverance in a competition. By consistently modeling these actions, you set a practical standard for your child to emulate both on and off the mats.

CONFIDENCE AND HUMILITY

In Jiu-Jitsu, confidence and humility grow hand in hand. Confidence comes alive when children face challenges head-on, like landing a tricky technique or stepping into their first competition with determination. But it's humility that teaches them the true art of learning—to value the guidance of their coaches, respect the efforts of their teammates, and find lessons in their struggles. Together, these qualities prepare children to navigate the highs and lows of life with strength and perspective.

As parents, we have the privilege of supporting this balance. Confidence doesn't mean avoiding failure, it means enjoying the process, trying again, and appreciate every little progress. Humility reminds us all that growth is endless, that every experience—win or lose—teaches something valuable. By nurturing both, we help our children see that strength is not just about believing in themselves but also about recognizing the value in others.

Practical Tips:

Celebrate Confidence: Highlight how confidence evolve from small victories and steady progress. For example, "I loved how you tackled that math problem today—it reminded me of how you stayed calm and focused during your drills last week."

Humility and Teamwork: Emphasize moments where humility builds stronger relationships. For instance, "I saw how you asked your teammate for help during that drill—it takes real character to trust and learn from others."

Confidence & Humility: Share your own moments of balancing these traits. For example, "At work today, I had to present an idea I wasn't sure about. I asked my colleague for feedback, and it helped me so much to make my plan better." This shows how the two values complement each other.

PRACTICAL TIPS FOR PARENTS

Connect the Dots: Guide your child to recognize how lessons from Jiu-Jitsu apply to other situations. For example, link the discipline needed for consistent training to completing homework or the problem-solving in sparring to overcoming a tricky situation with a friend. This bridges their understanding of Jiu-Jitsu values to everyday life.

Foster Self-Reflection: Encourage your child to think deeply about their progress. Ask questions like, "What's a challenge you've faced in training, and how did you overcome it?" or "How has learning this skill helped you outside of the gym?" These reflections connect their experiences on the mats to their character as a whole.

Be Patient: Recognize that building character, just like mastering techniques, takes time. Celebrate small but meaningful steps, such as showing respect to a teammate or pushing through a tough drill. These moments form the foundation of progressive improvements.

CONCLUSION FOR THE SECTION

The lessons your child learns through Jiu-Jitsu extend far beyond the mat, influencing how they handle schoolwork, navigate friendships, and approach challenges with determination and creativity. By actively participating in their journey and practicing discipline, problem-solving, and self-reflection at home, you're deepening your connection with your child while guiding them to become confident, grounded individuals ready to face life's challenges with courage and insight.

"The ultimate aim

of martial arts

lies not in victory

nor defeat,

but in the perfection

of the character

of its participants."

- Gichin Funakoshi

YOUR FEEDBACK MATTERS

Thank you for reading *The Jiu Jitsu Parents*. If you enjoy this book, I would be truly grateful if you could take a moment to leave a review on Amazon.

Your feedback not only helps others discover the book, but also supports my continued work as an author.

Scan the QR code below to go directly to the review page:

or visit:
https://www.amazon.com/review/create-review?
asin=B0DWDM44H9

With appreciation Philippe Eggert

Part C:
Supporting Youth Athletes

INTRODUCTION

As your child's passion for Jiu-Jitsu grows, so does the level of commitment required to support them. Transitioning from recreational practice to becoming a more serious youth athlete is both thrilling and demanding. It's a stage where training intensifies, competition pressures increase, and the stakes—both emotional and physical—rise higher.

As parents, this phase will challenge us in new ways. We might find ourselves juggling travel schedules, tournament expenses, and the ever-present desire to see our child succeed. The whirlwind of competition, expectations, and dreams of medals can easily consume our focus. But it's in this stage, perhaps more than any other, that our role as supportive parents becomes critical.

Supporting a youth athlete goes far beyond winning medals or achieving personal bests. It's about fostering their mental strength, maintaining balance in their lives, and helping them develop the skills that truly matter. It's about guiding them through the inevitable highs and lows of competitive sports in a way that leaves their love for Jiu-Jitsu—and their sense of self—intact.

This part of the book is written to help you navigate the unique challenges and responsibilities of raising a youth athlete. And believe me when I say—I know what it takes. Together, we'll explore how to manage the demands of training and competition, balance school with recovery, and support your child emotionally. This includes helping them set realistic goals, navigate setbacks, and embrace a mindset focused on long-term development over short-term wins.

Remember, it is a marathon, not a sprint.

Let this serve as a reminder that your role as a parent is not to shape a champion, but to nurture a well-rounded individual. By supporting their aspirations while keeping their love for the journey intact, you are helping build not just a skilled athlete, but a compassionate person ready to face life's challenges.

10. UNDERSTANDING THE COMMITMENT OF YOUTH ATHLETES:

As your child's dedication to Jiu-Jitsu grows, it becomes more than just an activity—it starts shaping their sense of identity and daily routines. For youth athletes, Jiu-Jitsu becomes a way of life, requiring a delicate balance of long training sessions, competition preparation, school responsibilities, and maintaining social connections with friends and family.

As a parent, your role transforms during this stage. It's no longer just about supporting their participation but about working together to manage the growing demands of their athletic journey, ensuring they feel supported both practically and emotionally. From logistical planning to emotional support, your role becomes essential in helping them maintain balance and perspective while pursuing their passion.

TRAINING SCHEDULES
AND BALANCING SCHOOLWORK

For youth athletes, balancing an intensive training schedule with the demands of school is a challenge, but it's also an opportunity to learn how to manage time more effectively. Helping your child find this balance is about working together and showing them that with teamwork and a little creativity, even the busiest days can be successfully managed. Your encouragement helps them feel supported, not just in their Jiu-Jitsu journey, but in understanding how teamwork and good time management can build confidence to handle school and life with a positive mindset. By staying connected to their needs— whether it's checking in on how they feel or adjusting plans together—you create an environment where they can manage these responsibilities with confidence and still find joy in the process.

Practical Tip:

Create a Shared Schedule: Sit down with your child and plan their week together, making time for training, schoolwork, friends, playtime and even moments to relax. Using a visual planner, like a whiteboard or calendar, can help them maintain the overview and feel confident and organized.

Prioritize Rest and Recovery: Highlight the importance of rest by helping your child create bedtime routines that serve them and include off days in their schedule. Remind them that taking time to recover not only boosts their energy but also supports steady progress and prevents injuries and overtraining.

Support Study Habits: Create together a calm and distraction-free study space, such as the kitchen table or a favorite quiet corner. Guide them in breaking larger assignments into smaller, achievable pieces and encourage focused study times with short breaks to keep their energy and motivation high.

FINANCIAL AND TIME INVESTMENT

Supporting a youth athlete requires a realistic understanding of the financial and time commitments involved. Tournament fees, travel expenses, and the cost of additional gear can quickly add up. Weekends spent traveling to competitions further increase the commitment. However, these challenges also open doors to bonding with your child and create opportunities for important lessons about responsibility, prioritization, gratitude, and teamwork. By planning thoughtfully and involving your child, you can make these commitments more rewarding for both of you.

Practical Tip:

Plan Ahead: Create a yearly competition calendar and a detailed budget that includes competition fees, travel costs, and equipment expenses. A clear plan gives you a better understanding of the expenses ahead, helping you manage the financial realities and plan the trips earlier, which can help you save on costs.

Involve Your Child: Have open conversations about how these commitments affect the family budget and involve them in prioritizing expenses. For instance, discuss how saving in one area can help fund tournament trips. This approach fosters responsibility and appreciation for the effort required.

Maximize Time Together: Use travel and downtime during competitions to strengthen your relationship with your child. Whether it's sharing stories, exploring a local landmark, or finding a cool lunch spot, these times can become cherished memories and opportunities to deepen your connection.

Youth athletes face significant emotional challenges alongside the physical demands of their sport. The pressure to perform well at tournaments, the disappointment of a tough loss, and the frustration when progress feels slow are all part of their journey. These moments can weigh heavily on their young shoulders. As a parent, our role is far more than just being on the sidelines—it's about being their unwavering support system. By noticing small signals—like the way they let their head hang after a tough match or the joy in their voice when they master a new technique—you show them they're seen and understood. This trust grows when they know they can share both their frustrations and their triumphs without being judged, creating a foundation of trust and confidence to help them navigate the ups and downs faithfully.

Practical Tip:

Check in Regularly: Create consistent moments to ask how they're feeling about their training or competitions. Simple, open-ended questions like, "What was the best experience at practice this week?" or "What's been frustrating lately?" can encourage them to share freely.

Provide Encouragement: Recognize the emotional weight your child carries when setbacks or slow progress occur. Validate their feelings and let them know it's okay to feel disappointed or frustrated. Instead of jumping to solutions, simply being there to listen can provide the reassurance they need to move forward.

Be Their Anchor: When emotions run high—after a tough loss or a difficult week—offer them a steady, calming presence. Reassure them by acknowledging their hard work and dedication, reminding them that your pride is in who they are, not just what they achieve.

CELEBRATING MILESTONES

In the busy life of a youth athlete, taking time to celebrate achievements—whether it's mastering a difficult technique, staying committed to training, or displaying great sportsmanship—acknowledges their effort and dedication in meaningful ways. These moments not only boost their confidence but also remind them of the joy and fulfillment that comes from their hard work.

Practical Tip:

Make It Special: Celebrate in a way that reflects your child's personality. Whether it's a quiet movie night, their favorite meal, or a thoughtful token of appreciation, these moments show you truly value their hard work and dedication.

Highlight Effort Over Results: Celebrate their commitment by marking milestones like attending every practice during a tough month or showing determination in competition, regardless of the outcome. Celebrate these efforts by creating a small tradition, like framing a photo from a special moment or giving them a keepsake tied to their achievement. These gestures make milestones memorable and reinforce their hard work in a tangible way.

Be Realistic About Commitments: As a parent, recognize the level of dedication required to support a youth athlete. Reflect on how much time, energy, and resources you can realistically commit, and plan accordingly. Being honest with yourself about these demands helps ensure that your involvement remains sustainable and positive for both you and your child.

Support Their Goals: Understand that your commitment as a parent plays a vital role in helping your child achieve their dreams. Reflect on the sacrifices and adjustments you're willing to make, ensuring they align with your family's overall balance and priorities. By understanding the broader commitment, you can better support their goals without unintentionally imposing your own expectations.

Stay Flexible: Recognize that the journey of a youth athlete is dynamic and ever-changing. Be prepared to adapt your level of involvement as schedules and priorities shift, such as stepping back during exam periods or stepping up to support them through a demanding competition cycle. Flexibility ensures that your support evolves alongside their needs, creating a partnership that strengthens their growth and commitment.

Conclusion for the Section:

Supporting a youth athlete means to fully commit to the unique challenges and responsibilities that come with this role. It's not just about logistics and finances —it's about fully understanding the sacrifices that come with supporting your child as they walk this path. Your commitment—in time, resources, and emotional presence—provides the foundation for them to pursue their dream of being an athlete.

By recognizing what this demands from you as a parent and embracing it with intention, you demonstrate the value of dedication. Together, you and your child will build a partnership grounded in trust and mutual respect, ensuring that the lessons of Jiu-Jitsu shape not only their athletic journey but also your shared connection.

"Success isn't always

about greatness.

It's about consistency.

Consistent hard work

leads to success.

Greatness will come."

- Dwayne Johnson

11. COMPETITION SUPPORT

For youth athletes, tournaments and competitions are the highlights of their annual calendar. They represent more than just matches—they are moments where hard work, dedication, and passion come together. Competitions are thrilling, but they also bring challenges, blending excitement with moments of uncertainty.

As a parent, your presence is a steady anchor during these events. By helping your child prepare with care, offering calm reassurance on the day, you help not just their performance but their growth, in every aspect of their development.

PREPARING FOR COMPETITIONS

Preparation for a tournament extends beyond physical training. It's about creating a sense of readiness and calm that enables your child to step onto the mat with confidence. By working together, you can transform preparation into a meaningful and supportive experience.

Practical Tip:

Understand the Rules: Take time to review the tournament rules with your child. Knowing how points are scored, what moves are allowed, the weigh in regulations, and any specific competition guidelines ensures they feel prepared and confident.

Discuss a Game Plan: Collaborate with their coach to outline a match strategy, like preferred positions, takedowns, guards, sweeps, top button game, what submissions to go for. A clear plan reduces uncertainty and builds focus.

Pack Together: Involve your child in preparing their competition bag. Essentials include a spare Gi, snacks, water, and a comfort item (like a favorite hoodie or playlist). This shared task helps them feel organized and in control.

Familiarize Them with the Venue: If possible, review details about the competition location in advance or show them photos to ease their nerves. Knowing what to expect can significantly boost their excitement.

SUPPORTING EMOTIONAL BALANCE ON THE DAY

Competition day can feel like an emotional rollercoaster—a day where both you and your child share the excitement, nerves, and anticipation. Your child may look to you for reassurance in moments of doubt or uncertainty. These emotions are completely normal and show how much it means to them. Your role is to be that steady presence, offering them balance and helping them enjoy the experience with a positive and calm mindset.

Practical Tip:

Pre-Match Reset Rituals: Help your child develop simple routines to calm their nerves, such as bouncing lightly on their toes, taking deep breaths, or repeating positive self-talk like, "I've got this." These rituals can center them and boost their confidence.

Stay Calm, Stay Positive: Your energy influences your child's energy. When you stay calm and positive, your child naturally feels safe. This is known as the "transfer of energy" in psychology. Practice deep breathing to ground yourself in the moment and project calmness and confidence.

"What's Your Next Move?" Thinking: During competition, emotions can cloud focus. Encourage your child to pause and take a deep breath when it starts to overthink. Help them refocus by asking simple, grounding questions like, "What's one thing you can control right now?" This helps them stay present and shift their mindset toward problem-solving instead of feeling overwhelmed.

HANDLING WINS AND LOSSES

How you respond to your child's wins and losses shapes how they experience their results. Celebrate their effort, guide them through the emotions of tough matches, and help them find balance between the pride of winning and the perspective to learn from losses. By focusing on meaningful moments—like a handshake with their opponent regardless the outcome or reflecting on what they've learned from this tournament—you can turn every experience into an opportunity and a positive process of learning and growth.

Practical Tip:

"Thank You" Routine: After every match, encourage your child to thank their opponent and their coach. If they forget, gently remind them by saying, "Let's go thank your opponent for the match." This small, consistent act builds humility and reinforces the importance of respect, win or lose. Over time, it becomes second nature, fostering a sense of gratitude both on and off the mat.

Celebrate the Wins with Growth in Mind: After a win, guide your child to reflect on what led to their success. You might say, "That was a great match! What do you think made the difference?" This keeps the focus on effort and preparation while helping them recognize areas to continue improving. Celebrating the journey rather than just the result nurtures a balanced and humble mindset.

Reframe the Losses with Care: After a tough loss, focus on creating a safe space for your child to process their emotions. Rather than jumping into analysis, acknowledge their effort by saying, "I know that was a hard match—you gave it your all." Later, when they're ready, gently guide them to reflect with questions like, "What's one thing you learned?" or "What would you try differently next time?" This approach helps them see losses as part of their growth, not as a setback.

For a dedicated youth athlete, competitions are much more than just events—they're the moments where their passion and hard work come to life. These days carry excitement and nerves, but they're also where your child unfolds their potential. As a parent, you have an important role: Focus on the joy of competing and the love of challenges. Celebrate the new friendships they build and the lessons they earned from each match. By being present and maintaining a positive atmosphere, you help your child see these moments as more than just a competition day—they're part of the journey that makes their Jiu-Jitsu experience so meaningful.

Practical Tip:

Celebrate Small Rituals: Create pre-competition habits that bring comfort and excitement. This might be having a favorite breakfast, listening to a playlist they love, or taking a family photo at the weigh in. These small but meaningful gestures turn competition days into cherished traditions.

Encourage Social Connections: Tournaments are not just about individual performance—they're a chance to embrace the team spirit and the friendships that make Jiu-Jitsu special. Motivate your child to cheer for their teammates, share gratitude with competitors, or simply enjoy being part of the supportive community around the sport.

Add a Learning Moment: Competitions are an excellent opportunity for your child to learn through observation. Use downtime to watch other matches together and discuss techniques or strategies they find interesting. Encouraging curiosity helps them appreciate the sport's depth and keeps the day engaging beyond their own matches.

REFLECTING POST-TOURNAMENT

After a competition, reflection is a key part of growing as a young competitor. It's not just about what happened during the matches—it's about what they learned, how they felt, and what they want to build on. By reflecting on their performance, youth athletes can identify what worked, what challenged them, and how to prepare for their next tournament with focus and confidence.

Practical Tip:

Break Down Key Matches: Encourage your child to analyze specific moments in their matches. Ask: "What's the decisions you made that worked really well?" "What was the hardest moment, and how did you handle it?" "What's something you want to practice more for next time?" These questions help them focus on learning and improvement.

Competition Journal: Help your child to start a match journal for sorting their thoughts after each tournament. Suggest they jot down: Techniques and strategies they felt worked good for them. Situations that surprised or challenged them or made them struggle. Things they want to work on for their next competition. Over time, this record becomes a valuable tool for growth and motivation.

Celebrate Small Victories: Highlight the specific decisions and strategies that led to success, like maintaining control during a difficult moment or executing a well-practiced technique. Share observations such as: "I saw how you adapted in that second match—that showed great focus." "You kept pushing even when things got tough—that's something to be proud of." This shifts the focus from outcomes to effort and personal growth.

PRACTICAL TIPS FOR PARENTS

Be Prepared for Ups and Downs: Tournament days can bring unexpected challenges, like a last-minute schedule change or a tough loss. Stay adaptable by focusing on how your child feels in the moment, offering encouragement, and reminding them that these experiences are part of the journey.

Use Downtime Wisely: While tournament schedules are often packed, look for small moments between matches to help your child reset. Encourage them to take a few deep breaths, hydrate, review their game plan, or share a quick, lighthearted conversation. These brief resets can keep their mindset positive, focused, and mentally prepared for the next match.

Keep the Big Picture in Mind: Remind your child that every competition is just a part of their larger Jiu-Jitsu journey. Highlight how each match—win or lose—helps them grow, learn, and improve, keeping the focus on their passion for the sport and the joy of competing.

Conclusion for the Section:

Competitions offer so much more than just a chance to win—they're where your child's dedication and courage shine. By supporting them through the highs and lows, helping them find meaning in the experience, and celebrating the small victories along the way, you're fostering their confidence and love for the sport. These moments reinforce the values of Jiu-Jitsu, shaping their growth and building their confidence.

"You either win

or you learn."

- Carlos Gracie Jr.

12. HELPING YOUR CHILD SET GOALS

Goal setting is a vital part of your child's Jiu-Jitsu journey, especially as they advance into youth athletics. Clear goals provide direction and motivation, helping them focus and measure their progress. However, the most meaningful goals are realistic, flexible, and driven by your child's own aspirations—not external pressures.

As a parent, your role is to guide and support them in creating goals that resonate with their interests and passions. It's about encouraging their independence while offering a steady presence to cheer them on every step of the way.

ENCOURAGING SELF-DRIVEN GOALS

The most meaningful goals are those that come from within. When your child sets their own aspirations, they feel a stronger sense of ownership, which naturally fosters commitment and motivation.

Practical Tip:

Ask Open-Ended Questions: Encourage your child to explore what excites or challenges them in their training. For example, ask, "What's one thing you'd love to improve during practice?" or "What's a skill you'd like to use in your next matches?"

Reflect Together: If they seem unsure, guide them by highlighting their strengths and areas for growth.

For instance, "You've been really consistent with your takedowns—how about working on improving your finishes next?"

By keeping the focus on their interests and letting them take the lead, you're empowering them to set goals that truly resonate with their journey.

BALANCING SHORT-TERM AND LONG-TERM GOALS

Striking a balance between immediate, achievable goals and bigger aspirations is key to keeping your child motivated. Short-term goals provide a sense of accomplishment, while long-term ones help them envision their potential and stay focused on the journey.Striking a balance between immediate, achievable goals and bigger aspirations is key to keeping your child motivated. Short-term goals provide a sense of accomplishment, while long-term ones help them envision their potential and stay focused on the journey. This balance teaches your child that growth is a process made up of small, meaningful steps that contribute to larger achievements. By understanding this, they learn to appreciate progress while staying connected to their long-term dreams.

As a parent of a youth athlete, you've likely seen how your child thrives on moments of progress—like improving their endurance in training or executing a new technique successfully during sparring. These short-term goals keep their energy focused and their spirits high. At the same time, these achievements act as stepping stones toward larger aspirations, such as competing at a higher level or refining their overall game. Your role is to help them stay present and celebrate these milestones while guiding their perspective toward the bigger picture.

When these goals align with your child's personal interests and abilities, they also build a sense of ownership over their journey. Short-term goals give them the satisfaction of seeing results and help maintain their enthusiasm, while long-term goals keep their vision forward-looking and purposeful. Think of it like building a puzzle together—each piece matters, and every time you place one, the bigger picture becomes clearer.

Practical Tip:

Break Big Goals into Steps: If your child has a large goal, like competing in a national or even international tournament, help them break it down into manageable milestones—such as perfecting specific techniques, building confidence in sparring, or mastering their game plan regarding the tournaments ruleset. Each step should feel attainable and directly contribute to the larger goal. For newer athletes, these steps might include smaller milestones like attending all scheduled training sessions for a month or asking their coach for feedback on specific areas of improvement.

Celebrate Milestones: Recognize their progress along the way. Whether it's nailing a tricky sweep or showing mental toughness during an intensive training session, celebrating these moments reinforces the importance of effort and consistency. Highlight the connection between these achievements and their long-term aspirations to make the process meaningful.

Support Goal Tracking: Help your child keep track of their progress by creating a simple visual chart or checklist. This could include small rewards for reaching milestones, such as a favorite activity or their favorite family dinner to acknowledge their effort. These practices keep the process collaborative and engaging.

By helping your child break down ambitious goals into actionable steps, you're not only guiding their growth as an athlete but also creating opportunities for meaningful personal victories. Each milestone they reach—whether it's understanding a new technique or showing determination through a tough training cycle—strengthens their confidence and mental toughness. These moments, supported by your steady encouragement, become the foundation for their success both in competition and in the challenges they'll face beyond the mat.

As your child's skills and interests evolve, their goals should grow with them. Flexibility is essential to keeping their journey engaging and aligned with their current aspirations. Adjusting goals ensures they remain motivated and excited about their progress. As they mature, their understanding of what they want to achieve often deepens, and their ambitions may shift toward new challenges—whether it's refining advanced techniques, competing at higher levels, or balancing their athletic aspirations with other personal goals.

Helping them adapt their goals isn't just about staying aligned with their interests; it's also about teaching them to embrace change as a natural part of growth. A rigid attachment to old goals can stifle progress, but learning to adjust and refocus fosters resilience and a growth-oriented mindset. By modeling this flexibility, you're showing them how to navigate shifts in priorities with confidence.

Practical Tip:

Check In Regularly: Schedule time every few months to revisit their goals. Ask reflective questions such as, "How do you feel about your tournament performance so far?" or "What's one skill you're proud of improving recently?" For youth athletes juggling other commitments, these conversations can help them stay balanced, motivated, and ensure their goals remain realistic and fulfilling.

Normalize Change: For example, if they initially aimed to compete in regional tournaments but now wish to focus on preparing for higher-stakes national or state competitions, celebrate this evolution. It reflects their growing ambition and deeper understanding of their capabilities. Collaborate with their coach to refine these new objectives, which might involve modifying their training schedule or planning for travel, to align with their evolving priorities.

By supporting their ability to adapt, you're equipping your child with a crucial life skill: the ability to navigate change with confidence. Whether they're refining their approach to training or pivoting to new aspirations, learning to adapt fosters self-awareness. This process doesn't just enhance their growth on the mat—it prepares them to tackle academic challenges, social shifts, and future ambitions with the same focus and determination.

AVOIDING THE TRAP
OF UNREALISTIC EXPECTATIONS

Dreaming big is wonderful, but overly ambitious goals can lead to frustration or discouragement—especially for young athletes navigating the competitive demands of Jiu-Jitsu. While it's natural to aspire to significant achievements, setting goals that feel unattainable can undermine your child's motivation and confidence. As a parent, your role is to guide them in finding a balance between challenging themselves and setting demanding but realistic, incremental targets.

Unrealistic expectations often stem from focusing too much on outcomes, like winning every tournament, without considering the developmental process required to get there. Redirecting attention to effort and progress rather than immediate results helps your child stay engaged and find joy in the journey. It's about creating a path that acknowledges both their current abilities and their aspirations, so they feel empowered and motivated to keep improving.

Practical Tip:

Assess Goals Together: Take time regularly to revisit your child's goals and ensure they align with their current skills and interests. Use open-ended questions like, "What's something you feel you're improving on lately?" or "Does this goal still feel exciting and within reach?" These conversations provide a chance to celebrate progress while identifying areas where expectations might need adjustment, keeping your child motivated and engaged.

Watch for Signs of Strain: Unrealistic expectations can show up in your child's emotional and physical responses. Notice if they seem unusually frustrated with themselves, withdraw from activities they usually enjoy, or lose the excitement they once had for training. These could be signs that their goals feel overwhelming. Open up a conversation to understand their perspective, asking questions like, "What part of training feels the hardest right now?" or "What makes you feel that way?" This allows you to collaboratively adjust expectations, ensuring they continue to feel supported and motivated.

By guiding your child toward realistic yet meaningful goals, you're fostering their love for Jiu-Jitsu while helping them develop a deeper sense of purpose and determination. This approach not only supports their growth on the mat but also equips them with the skills to navigate life's challenges with focus, adaptability, and confidence.

Your role in your child's goal-setting is to guide and encourage, not to take control. By giving them the space to set their own aspirations and take ownership, you're helping them develop valuable skills like self-motivation and accountability. At the same time, your steady presence as a supportive partner fosters confidence, creating a balance where they feel empowered but never alone.

Being a supportive partner doesn't mean removing challenges from their path—it means helping them see challenges as opportunities. Your encouragement is most impactful when it meets them where they are.

Practical Tip:

Encourage Ownership of Goals: Increase your child's sense of ownership by helping them reflect on their goals. Ask open-ended questions like, "What motivated you to set this goal?" or "What steps do you think will help you achieve it?" This approach helps them stay motivated and develop self-awareness in their journey.

Help Them Stay on Track: Motivation can waver, and that's when your support matters most. Gently remind them of their commitments by saying things like, "I know it feels tough now, but remember why you set this goal and how much progress you've already made." This approach helps them refocus and keeps their goals in perspective.

By being a collaborative partner in their goal-setting process, you're equipping your child with the tools to take ownership of their aspirations. This collaboration fosters self-discipline and confidence, while also teaching them to navigate challenges and celebrate progress with purpose.

PRACTICAL TIPS FOR PARENTS

Revisit and Refine Goals Together: Use regular check-ins to revisit your child's goals and refine them as needed. For example, ask, "What's something new you've learned recently that could help you adjust your direction?" or "Does this goal still feel exciting to you?" This process encourages self-reflection while maintaining alignment with their progress.

Support Clear and Achievable Goals: Help your child navigate the demands of competitive Jiu-Jitsu by breaking down ambitious objectives into manageable steps. For example, if they're preparing for a tournament, work with them to focus on specific training goals, such as improving takedowns or stamina. This ensures their efforts remain purposeful and aligned with their larger aspirations without feeling overwhelming.

Lead by Example: Share moments when you've adapted your own goals or faced challenges. For example, "When I had to adjust my plans at work, I realized focusing on small wins helped me keep going. You're doing the same with your training—it's amazing to see." By modeling adaptability, you reinforce the importance of persistence in their journey. For instance, "When I set a goal to improve my fitness, I started by focusing on consistent, small efforts—just like you're doing with your training. It's inspiring to see how committed you are to your goals."

Helping your child navigate and achieve meaningful goals is one of the most fulfilling aspects of being a Jiu-Jitsu parent. By fostering self-driven aspirations, celebrating their growth, and modeling persistence, you're giving them tools to succeed in all areas of life.

"The man who moves

a mountain

begins by carrying away

small stones."

- Confucius

13. NAVIGATING CHALLENGES
OF ADOLESCENCE
IN COMPETITIVE SPORTS

Parenting a teenager isn't easy, especially during the tumultuous years of adolescence. Add the ups and downs of competitive sports like Jiu-Jitsu, and the challenges can feel even more dynamic. These years are marked by rapid change—physically, emotionally, and socially. For teens dedicated to Jiu-Jitsu, this often means grappling with moments of self-doubt, external pressures from peers or competition, and continuously shifting motivation and interests.

As a parent, it's natural to feel uncertain about when to step in or give your teen space. This stage isn't about solving every challenge—it's about being a steady, supportive presence while empowering your teen to navigate their own path. These years are pivotal, not just for their growth in Jiu-Jitsu, but for shaping their identity, confidence, and balance they'll carry into adulthood

Throughout this section, we'll explore practical strategies to help your teen maintain their passion, navigate peer pressures, manage emotional swings, and balance the demands of Jiu-Jitsu with their evolving personal lives. Together, let's ensure that Jiu-Jitsu remains a positive, empowering outlet where they can thrive.

HELPING THEM STAY MOTIVATED
WHEN PASSION WAVERS

Teenagers often question their interests, even in activities they once loved like Jiu-Jitsu. It's not uncommon for them to come home frustrated after a tough session or wonder if all their hard work is paying off. These doubts often surface during adolescence, as slow progress, social pressures, or shifting priorities take center stage. For parents, these moments may feel disheartening, but they're also an opportunity to nurture growth and resilience.

Your role is to help your teen reconnect with their "why"—the spark that first drew them to Jiu-Jitsu. This could be as simple as reminiscing about the pride they felt after earning their first stripe or the joy of mastering a challenging technique. Honest, open conversations about these moments can remind them of the deeper purpose Jiu-Jitsu holds in their life.

Sometimes, seeing the sport through a fresh lens helps reignite their passion. Encourage them to try something new, like mentoring younger students in a kids' class or watching matches of their favorite athletes for inspiration. These shifts in perspective can reignite a sense of excitement and purpose.

Finally, let them know that it's okay to take a break. Adolescence is a time of exploration, and stepping away from the mats briefly doesn't mean they're giving up. Often, a short pause can help them recharge and come back with renewed enthusiasm.

Practical Tip:

Reignite Their "Why": Sit down with your teen to reflect on their journey in Jiu-Jitsu. Ask them about the moments that brought them the most pride or joy —whether it was the thrill of learning a new move, the camaraderie of their teammates, or the sense of achievement after a hard-fought match. Help them see how these experiences shaped their connection to the sport and explore ways to reignite that passion.

Explore Different Perspectives: Discuss new dimensions of Jiu-Jitsu to spark renewed interest. Encourage your teen to attend seminars, watch inspiring matches, or dive into instructional content that tickles their curiosity of advanced techniques and strategies. Alternatively, have them assist with younger students—passing on their knowledge can foster confidence, remind them of their own progress and how fare they already came, and offer a refreshing sense of purpose.

Normalize Breaks: Remind your teen that taking a short break is a natural part of any long-term journey. Frame it as an opportunity to recharge both physically and mentally, emphasizing that stepping away doesn't negate their commitment. Many athletes return to the mats with fresh perspectives and renewed enthusiasm after taking time to reflect and rest.

DEALING WITH HEIGHTENED SENSITIVITIES AND EMOTIONAL SWINGS

Teenagers often navigate a rollercoaster of emotional highs and lows, driven by the natural hormonal changes of adolescence. Adding the demands of training and competition can amplify these fluctuations, leaving them overwhelmed or unsure of themselves. A tough session might lead to feelings of frustration, while an intense tournament could shake their confidence. These swings, though difficult to navigate, are deeply rooted in their natural brain development. While challenging, emphasize the need for a steady, nonjudgmental presence where teens feel safe to express themselves. They may not always know how to articulate what they're feeling, but your calm guidance can help them begin to navigate these complex emotions.

As a parent, it's not always easy to watch your teen wrestle with these feelings. You might feel unsure of how much to step in or when to simply listen. Your calm presence can make all the difference. As a parent, it's natural to feel overwhelmed by your teen's emotions. You might wonder if you're saying the right things or worry about making the situation worse. Remember, your role isn't to fix every problem—it's to show that you're there, listening and supporting them through the highs and lows. Acknowledging their emotions without judgment helps them feel understood, while your guidance teaches them to navigate challenges constructively. By modeling patience and emotional steadiness yourself, you can turn these difficult moments into meaningful growth opportunities for your teen.

Practical Tip:

Help Them Name Their Feelings: When your teen seems upset, help them explore what they're feeling without pressure. For instance, 'It seems like today's session was tough—want to share what's on your mind?' creates space for openness and validation.

Validate Without Overreacting: Acknowledge their emotions with empathy while staying calm. Saying, 'I understand why that loss felt disappointing—what's one thing you feel proud of from today?' shifts the focus toward constructive reflection.

Model Emotional Resilience: Show them how setbacks are part of growth by sharing your own experiences. For example, 'I've had projects that felt impossible, but breaking them into smaller steps helped. You'll figure out your way forward too.' This demonstrates perseverance in a relatable way.

HELPING THEM NAVIGATE SOCIAL PRESSURES

The social dynamics of adolescence can be complicated, and being a dedicated athlete introduces another layer to their confusing world. Your teenager is trying to balance relationships with teammates, coaches, and competitors, while also navigating friendships and social expectations at school. These experiences can be incredibly valuable for developing social skills, empathy, and confidence, but they can also feel overwhelming at times. The emotional highs and lows of navigating these difficulties are normal. Your steady support can help them feel confident and secure as they navigate these challenges.

As a parent, your role is to provide guidance without overstepping. Encourage open conversations where they feel comfortable sharing their social experiences, both the good and the bad. Help them reflect on situations and explore ways to handle conflicts or challenging dynamics constructively.

Practical Tip:

Respect Their Boundaries: Teach your teen that it's okay to say "No, thank you" if they feel pushed into situations they're uncomfortable with—whether it's sparring too aggressively or taking on commitments they're not ready for. Empower them to advocate for themselves respectfully and confidently.

Encourage Supportive Connections: Help them understand the importance of surrounding themselves with teammates who uplift and challenge them in positive ways. Help them recognize the importance of surrounding themselves with teammates who uplift and challenge them in positive ways. By fostering these healthy relationships and embracing constructive competition, they can build confidence and a sense of belonging.

Be Their Safe Space: Let your teen know they can come to you with anything—whether it's a disagreement with a teammate or feelings of self-doubt. Remind them that it's okay to feel uncertain or vulnerable and that you're there to support them without judgment whenever they need it.

ADDRESSING BODY IMAGE CONCERNS
IN A HEALTHY WAY

Adolescence is a time when teens naturally become more aware of their bodies, and in a sport like Jiu-Jitsu—where weight classes and physical performance are emphasized—this awareness can sometimes lead to self-consciousness. As a parent, you can help your child develop a healthy and positive relationship with their body by focusing on its capabilities rather than its appearance.

If your child is cutting weight, it's important to consider how this might conflict with their natural growth patterns. During growth spurts, weight cutting can inhibit development. Encouraging them to compete at their natural weight and fostering a healthy relationship with food is often a better long-term approach. For instance, reducing carbohydrate intake in a balanced way can naturally decrease water retention and help manage weight without compromising growth or performance. Consulting with a nutritionist can also ensure these choices support their overall health and training goals.

Practical Tip:

Shift the Focus to Function, Not Form: Encourage your teen to see their body as a tool for mastering skills and achieving goals on the mat. Highlight specific examples, such as how their stamina improved during training or how they executed a challenging technique. By celebrating these functional aspects, you help them value growth and performance over appearance.

Watch for Warning Signs: Be mindful of behaviors that might indicate unhealthy habits, such as skipping meals, obsessing over weight, or withdrawing from training. If you observe these signs, approach the conversation with care. For example, you might say, 'I've noticed you've been skipping meals—how can we work together to support you and ensure you're feeling strong and healthy?'

Celebrate Strength and Skill: Take time to acknowledge your teen's progress and achievements, whether it's mastering a complex submission or showing persistence during a tough match. Regularly reminding them that their body enables these accomplishments reinforces a positive, empowering perspective.

TEACHING BALANCE AND PERSPECTIVE

For teens dedicated to competing in Jiu-Jitsu, their passion is often inspiring, but it can sometimes create an unbalanced focus on the sport. While their commitment is admirable, it's important to help them see how Jiu-Jitsu fits into a broader, more fulfilling life. Striking a balance between training, academics, friendships, and rest isn't about limiting their enthusiasm—it's about teaching them to grow as individuals while pursuing their goals. Your role as a parent is to guide them gently, helping them build habits that support their overall well-being and allow them to to become the best version of themself.

Practical Tip:

Reframe Rest as a Strategic Tool: Show your teen how rest isn't just about recovery—it's a part of their long-term strategy. Discuss how professional athletes prioritize rest to sharpen focus and avoid burnout, and help them plan recovery days into their routine, especially after tough training weeks.

Tie Jiu-Jitsu to Broader Identity: Support your teen in seeing themselves as more than just an athlete. For instance, discuss how the focus and determination they bring to Jiu-Jitsu can also help them excel in academics, connect with others, or explore creative projects. This broader perspective helps them balance passion with other areas of growth.

Teach Adaptability Through Reflection: After a tough match or practice, guide your teen in reflecting on what they learned—not just in technique but about themselves. For example, discuss how adapting during a match mirrors handling challenges at school or in friendships. These connections build confidence and a sense of purpose beyond the mat.

STRENGTHENING YOUR RELATIONSHIP THROUGH INDEPENDENCE

As teenagers develop, they naturally begin to seek more independence as part of their growth toward forming their own identity. This shift is a normal and necessary part of adolescence, but it can sometimes create moments of tension. As parents, we slowly need to let them go and give away the control over their life, which is a new, emotional, and challenging experience for us.

But independence doesn't mean letting go entirely—it's about giving your teen the space to explore and make their own decisions, knowing you're always there to support them when they need you. At this stage of their life, this is a chance to build real mutual respect by listening to their thoughts empathetically, accepting their goals, and showing trust in their choices. By maintaining an open and supportive relationship, you help them grow into confident, capable individuals while keeping the bond between you strong. This approach not only nurtures their independence but also reassures them that they have a secure foundation to rely on.

Practical Tip:

Be Their Supporter, Not Their Manager: Give your teen the freedom to take ownership of their responsibilities. For example, if they're preparing for a tournament, ask how you can support their process rather than stepping in with advice. This shows trust in their abilities while keeping the lines of communication open.

Check In Without Micromanaging: Show interest in their journey by asking thoughtful questions that encourage reflection. For instance, "What's something you're proud of from practice this week?" or "Is there anything you're finding challenging?" These conversations help your teen feel supported without feeling like their independence is being questioned.

Respect Their Choices and Celebrate Growth: Support your teen's decisions, even if they choose a different approach than you might expect. For instance, if they want to try a new training routine or set different goals, embrace their autonomy. Acknowledge their efforts and celebrate their milestones—both big and small—to strengthen their confidence and accountability.

Even as your teen begins to chart their own path and take greater ownership of their choices, your guidance remains invaluable. By offering support, trust, and encouragement, you ensure that their journey toward independence is grounded in a secure and loving relationship. Remember, your role as a steady presence in their life is just as important now as ever.

PRACTICAL TIPS FOR PARENTS

Stay Involved Without Overstepping: Your teen benefits from your guidance, but they also need room to make their own decisions. For instance, if they're preparing for a competition, ask how you can support their preparation instead of stepping in to manage it. This shows that you trust them while staying available when they need you.

Focus on Long-Term Growth: Shift the focus away from immediate results and emphasize the bigger picture. Talk with your teen about how the discipline they're building now will serve them far beyond Jiu-Jitsu, helping them handle challenges in school, relationships, and future endeavors.

Celebrate Who They're Becoming: Take time to recognize not just their achievements, but the qualities they're developing along the way. For example, highlight moments when they showed perseverance during a tough match or supported a teammate. Acknowledging these traits reinforces their growth as a person, not just an athlete.

Adolescence may be a time of transition, but it's also full of opportunities for growth. By offering thoughtful support and fostering open communication, you're guiding your child toward becoming a confident, self-reliant individual—ready to take on the challenges life throws at them.

.

"Life is like riding a bicycle.

To keep your balance,

you must keep moving."

- Albert Einstein

14. SUPPORTING MENTAL AND EMOTIONAL RESILIENCE

Competing in Jiu Jitsu challenges your child in ways that extend far beyond physical techniques. It's a journey of emotional and mental growth, teaching resilience as they face setbacks, problem-solve under pressure, and navigate moments of self-doubt. Resilience is about more than toughness—it's about adaptability, emotional awareness, and the courage to learn from every experience.

As parents, we play a crucial role in shaping this resilience. By fostering an environment where challenges are opportunities for growth and where emotions are met with understanding, we empower our children to build the skills they need to thrive. The following subsections explore how to guide your child in embracing problem-solving, normalizing failure, and developing emotional awareness, creating a foundation for resilience that will serve them both on and off the mats.

For youth athletes in Jiu-Jitsu, problem-solving takes on a sharper edge. Beyond escaping tricky positions, competitive athletes face challenges like refining strategies under pressure, analyzing performance after a match, and making quick adjustments during tournaments. These skills don't just help them succeed in competition—they build the critical thinking and adaptability that will serve them throughout life.

Practical Tip:

Encourage Match Reflection: After a tournament or sparring session, guide your child in breaking down what went well and what could improve. Ask questions like, "What's one decision you made that worked really well?" or "What's something you might try differently next time?" This helps them analyze outcomes constructively.

Foster Strategic Thinking: Work with their coach to help them identify areas of focus, like specific techniques or match strategies. For example, "How can you use your guard more effectively against taller opponents?" keeps problem-solving tied to actionable steps.

Model Problem-Solving Under Pressure: Share examples of how you've approached challenges with composure, such as, "When I felt stuck at work, I focused on one small change I could make, and it helped me move forward." Relating this to their Jiu-Jitsu journey makes the lesson more relatable.

Celebrate Creative Solutions: Highlight moments when your child thinks outside the box. For instance, if they use an unexpected sweep or a clever tactic to counter a strong opponent, praise their ingenuity: "That was a great adjustment—you really adapted to the situation."

NORMALIZING FAILURE AS PART OF GROWTH

For youth athletes, especially those active in competition, losses can feel demoralizing—a weight that threatens their confidence and passion. However, failure is not a reason to give up; it's a stepping stone to progress. Each mistake on the mat is an opportunity to analyze, adapt, and improve. By guiding your child to see losses and setbacks as part of their learning process, you help them develop a mindset that values effort and progress over perfection.

Normalizing failure also teaches an essential truth about competition: even the greatest champions face losses. What sets them apart is their ability to reflect, adjust, and persevere. While setbacks are opportunities, it's also important to validate your child's feelings in the moment, letting them process disappointment before focusing on progress. When your child begins to see mistakes as essential steps toward mastery, they can reframe challenges as chances to uncover hidden strengths and refine their approach. This mindset empowers them to face obstacles with determination and curiosity, turning setbacks into stepping stones for infinite growth.

Practical Tip:

Personalize with Stories: Share relatable examples of setbacks you've overcome, like a professional challenge or missed opportunity. Focus on how persistence and reflection led to growth, showing your child that failure is a universal experience.

Empower Reflection: After a loss or setback, guide your child to analyze the experience constructively. Ask questions like, "What's one thing you learned from that match?" or "What's one thing you want to try differently next time?" This helps them shift focus from disappointment to improvement.

Celebrate Incremental Growth: Recognize small wins in the learning process, such as improving a specific technique or showing more dedication during sparring. Highlighting progress reinforces their belief in steady improvement.

Frame Failure as Temporary: Encourage your child to view setbacks as part of a larger journey. Remind them that even the best athletes have faced challenges and that each step back is temporary if approached with determination.

BUILDING EMOTIONAL AWARENESS

For youth athletes, emotional awareness is the foundation for mental clarity and consistent performance. In the high-pressure world of competition, understanding and managing emotions like frustration, nervousness, or disappointment can shape how they develop confidence and sustain their passion for the sport. Helping your child to recognize their feelings and respond constructively equips them with the tools to stay composed under pressure and recover quickly from setbacks.

Emotional awareness is not just about identifying feelings—it's about building the confidence to face them without fear. When young athletes learn to process their emotions, they gain clarity and focus, which helps them make better decisions. By fostering an environment where emotions are acknowledged and respected, you empower your child to approach challenges with a calm, solution-oriented mindset, reinforcing their mental toughness and adaptability.

Practical Tip:

Turn Emotion into Insight: After a challenging match or training session, guide your child through their emotions by asking reflective questions like, "What felt hardest today, and why?" or "What could you try differently next time?" This helps them see emotions as part of their growth process.

Model Composure: Show your child how you manage your own emotions during tough situations. For example, say, "I felt overwhelmed earlier, so I took a few breaths to calm down and think clearly." This models emotional regulation in real time.

Celebrate Emotional Growth: Recognize when your child processes their feelings constructively, such as staying calm during a match or expressing their frustration thoughtfully. For example, "I saw how you stayed focused even when things got tough—that was a great way to handle the pressure."

Develop Emotional Check-Ins: Encourage your child to take brief moments during practice or matches to pause and ask themselves, "How am I feeling right now?" Teaching them to identify and name their emotions helps create self-awareness and a proactive approach to managing stress.

ENCOURAGING A GROWTH MINDSET

In Jiu-Jitsu, a growth mindset shapes how young athletes tackle challenges—not as roadblocks, but as stepping stones to mastery. This perspective encourages them to embrace the process of learning, whether it's refining a difficult technique, analyzing what went wrong after a loss, or persevering through plateaus. Instead of focusing solely on outcomes, they begin to value the effort, adaptability, and incremental progress that lead to long-term success.

Helping your child adopt this mindset means showing them that improvement isn't always immediate and that every setback carries lessons worth discovering. For example, struggling with a technique can teach patience and creativity, while a loss can inspire strategic adjustments. By connecting these moments to their growth, you instill a sense of purpose and determination that extends beyond the mat. As parents, leading by example and reinforcing these values in everyday situations can make the growth mindset a natural part of their journey.

Practical Tip:

Praise Effort Over Results: Recognize the hard work they put in, regardless of the outcome. For example, "I can see how much effort you've been putting into your guard passes—it's really paying off. Your focus on technique is showing progress."

Reframe "I Can't" with "Not Yet": When they express frustration, gently shift their perspective by saying, "You might not have it yet, but every attempt gets you closer." Tie this to a recent example, such as, "Remember how that sweep felt impossible last month, and now you're using it in sparring?"

Highlight Effort Stories: Share specific examples of perseverance—whether it's from a match they've improved in, a coach's journey overcoming challenges, or a professional athlete's persistence. For instance, "Your coach once said it took him a full year to master that same guard pass. Look how much closer you are after just a few months."

As a parent of a youth athlete, finding the right balance between offering support and encouraging independence can be a delicate process. This means knowing when to guide your child through challenges and when to step back, allowing them to make their own decisions and learn from their experiences. Striking this balance helps them build confidence, develop problem-solving skills, and grow into self-reliant individuals.

This balance doesn't mean stepping away entirely— it's about creating an environment where your child feels empowered to take ownership of their journey while knowing they can rely on you when ever needed. Whether it's discussing training goals, navigating competition nerves, or processing setbacks, your steady presence reassures them while fostering their independence.

Practical Tip:

Step Back, but Stay Close: Allow them to take the lead on decisions about training or competition strategies. For example, let them decide how to approach their next sparring session while remaining available to discuss their plans if they ask for input.

Encourage Self-Reflection: After matches or training sessions, ask open-ended questions like, "What do you think you did well today?" or "What's one area you want to improve next week?" This helps them develop critical thinking and self-awareness.

Celebrate Their Autonomy: Recognize moments where they show independence or handle challenges on their own. For example, "I noticed how you adjusted your technique during sparring—that was a smart move." Highlighting these moments reinforces their confidence and decision-making skills.

Resist Over-Solving Problems: When they encounter a challenge, resist the urge to solve it for them. Instead, ask, "What have you already tried?" or "What do you think you could do differently?" This encourages them to develop their own solutions while knowing you're there to support them.

RECOGNIZING WHEN TO SEEK EXTRA SUPPORT

There are moments in every youth athlete's journey where challenges can feel overwhelming—moments where their confidence or motivation may waver. As a parent, recognizing these times and knowing when to seek extra support is a crucial part of fostering their growth. Asking for help is not a sign of weakness; it's a vital skill that empowers both parents and children to navigate obstacles together.

Sometimes, your child may face struggles that feel too big to overcome alone, such as frustrations with plateaued progress, emotional stress from competition, or difficulties balancing training with other aspects of their life. Reaching out to trusted sources like their coach, teammates, other parents, or specialized professionals can provide fresh perspectives and tools to guide them through these challenges. By building a network of support, you reinforce the message that seeking help is a sign of strength and an important part of personal growth.

Practical Tip:

Notice the Signs: If your child shows signs of stress, such as withdrawal, anxiety, or a sudden lack of interest in training, take time to check in with them. Sharing your observations with their coach or a trusted mentor can provide valuable insights into their mindset and performance.

Reframe Asking for Help: Emphasize that seeking support is a strength, not a weakness. For example, say, "Even the best athletes have coaches and mentors to help them grow. It's how we all improve." Normalize this mindset to help your child feel more comfortable asking for help.

Leverage Peer Support: Encourage your child to connect with teammates or friends who have faced similar struggles. Peer encouragement often feels more relatable and can foster a sense of camaraderie and shared experience.

Model Help-Seeking Behavior: Share moments from your own life when seeking advice or guidance made a positive difference. For instance, "I was struggling with a work challenge, and asking a colleague for help gave me a new perspective." This demonstrates that asking for help is a valuable and normal part of growth.

PRACTICAL TIPS FOR PARENTS

Be a Role Model: Show your child how you navigate challenges by seeking support when needed. For instance, share moments when asking for advice helped you overcome a problem. This normalizes seeking help as a valuable and empowering step.

Focus on Their Worth: Remind your child regularly that their value isn't tied to wins or losses but rooted in their effort, growth, and character. For example, highlight moments when they showed great effort or teamwork, reinforcing these qualities over outcomes.

Celebrate Progress: Acknowledge even small signs of growth, such as their ability to handle competition nerves or take constructive feedback from a coach. Celebrate these milestones as meaningful parts of their larger journey, emphasizing how each step builds their confidence and skills.

Supporting your child's mental and emotional development doesn't mean solving every problem for them. It's about teaching them to recognize when to seek guidance and how to embrace challenges with confidence. By encouraging self-awareness, a growth mindset, and collaborative problem-solving, you help them develop skills that will serve them in Jiu-Jitsu and every other aspect of life.

"Do not pray for an easy life,

pray for the strength

to endure a difficult one."

- Bruce Lee

15. FOSTERING LEADERSHIP AND RESPONSIBILITY

As youth athletes progress in their Jiu-Jitsu journey, opportunities to step into leadership roles naturally arise. These moments—whether it's helping a new teammate learn a technique, demonstrating respect during training, or taking on responsibilities in the gym—become defining experiences. They teach young practitioners not only how to lead but also how to embody qualities like empathy, accountability, and humility.

In Jiu-Jitsu, leadership is not about being the best or the most accomplished competitor. It's about passing on skills and knowledge in meaningful ways. By teaching a teammate how to escape a position or sharing tips they've learned through experience, young leaders deepen their connection to the art. The young athlete who takes the time to guide a teammate through a challenging drill, or who shows discipline and focus during a tough session, learns that true leadership is about service—lifting others and contributing to a shared culture of growth.

By encouraging your child to recognize and embrace these moments of leadership, you can help them develop confidence and character. Highlight the impact their actions can have on others, and reinforce the importance of respect and teamwork as core values. As parents, we have the unique ability to shape how our children view leadership—not as a position of authority, but as a responsibility to uplift and inspire. These lessons extend far beyond the mat, equipping them with the tools to inspire and grow alongside their peers while preparing for life's challenges.

ENCOURAGING LEADERSHIP IN THE GYM

As young athletes progress, they naturally become role models for their peers, often without realizing it. Parents play a crucial role in helping their children recognize and embrace these responsibilities for leadership. Leadership is not about taking control but about being a good example through actions— helping teammates, showing respect, and contributing to the team's shared growth.

Leadership in the gym takes shape in many ways. It could be guiding a newer teammate through a challenging drill, staying after practice to assist with clean-up, or demonstrating patience when helping others understand techniques. These actions build responsibility, empathy, and a deeper understanding of the art while fostering a sense of belonging within the team.

By guiding your child to embrace these opportunities, you help them develop the qualities of a true leader—patience, empathy, and a commitment to lifting others.

Practical Tip:

Recognize Leadership Moments: Encourage your child to notice when they can step up to support others. For example, "If you see a teammate struggling with a technique, offer to help them work on it." Recognizing these moments fosters awareness and initiative.

Teaching Opportunities: Suggest that your child assist younger or less experienced teammates during drills. For example, if they've mastered a sweep, encourage them to share what worked for them. Teaching reinforces their understanding while helping others feel supported.

Leadership Through Actions: Discuss how simple acts, like guiding teammates during sparring or taking initiative to welcome new teammates, contribute to the team's success. These behaviors show that leadership is about consistent contributions, not titles or recognition.

BUILDING RESPONSIBILITY
THROUGH TRAINING

Leadership begins with personal accountability. Taking ownership of their training journey teaches your child discipline, self-reliance, and confidence. These moments are where true growth happens. It's not just about mastering techniques; it's about preparing thoughtfully, setting meaningful goals, and reflecting on the effort they're putting in every step of the way.

When your child approaches training with purpose and accountability, they'll begin to see how their actions directly shape their outcomes. Helping them embrace these responsibilities shows them that consistent effort is the foundation for progress and success. Your guidance can make all the difference in helping them build habits that last a lifetime.

Practical Tip:

Ownership of Preparation: Encourage your child to take responsibility for their training preparations. Let them pack their Gi and organize their gear. Guide them to think ahead and set specific intentions for sparring. For example, ask, "What's one technique or strategy you want to focus on during sparring today?" These habits not only build independence but also reinforce leadership by helping them take initiative.

Be Accountable to the Team: Highlight how their preparation and effort impact their teammates. For instance, remind them that showing up on time, being ready to drill, and staying focused contribute to a positive team environment. Leadership starts with taking responsibility for their role within the group.

Reflect on Responsibility: After training, encourage your child to reflect on moments when they took ownership of their progress. Ask questions like, "How did focusing on that technique help you today?" or "What's one thing you did to support your teammates during practice?" These discussions connect their actions to leadership and growth.

"Leadership is not about

being in charge.

It is about taking care

of those in your charge."

- Simon Sinek

HANDLING CONFLICTS WITH MATURITY

Leadership involves more than guiding others—it's about navigating conflicts with respect and composure. In the world of Jiu-Jitsu, problems can arise in many forms, whether it's a disagreement with a teammate, frustration during sparring, or the emotional challenges of a tough match. These moments offer invaluable opportunities for growth and reflection.

As a parent, you play a crucial role in helping your child build the emotional tools they need to handle conflicts maturely. It's not just about resolving the issue at hand but about fostering qualities like empathy, patience, and self-awareness. When your child learns to approach conflicts with a calm and constructive mindset, they not only strengthen their leadership abilities but also develop skills that will serve them throughout life.

Encouraging maturity in conflict resolution means guiding your child to see challenges as opportunities to grow. It's about teaching them to pause, reflect, and choose their actions thoughtfully rather than reacting impulsively. These lessons, practiced on the mats, create a foundation for handling disagreements with confidence and respect in every setting.

Practical Tip:

Practice Conflict Scenarios: Role-play specific situations together, such as how to approach a teammate after a misunderstanding during sparring or how to respond to an overly aggressive and emotional training partner. Use these scenarios to practice constructive language, such as, "I felt that was a bit too rough—can we tone it down?" These exercises help your child build confidence and prepare for real-life conflicts.

Encourage Respectful Communication: Teach your child how to address issues calmly and clearly. For example, phrases like, "Can we talk about what happened during sparring?" or "I felt you got very emotional—how can we avoid that next time?" provide them with practical tools for constructive discussions. Emphasize the importance of listening as well as speaking to understand others' perspectives.

Acknowledge Their Growth and Connect to Leadership: Recognize moments when they handle conflict with maturity and tie it to their leadership potential. For instance, say, "I saw how you talked to your teammate after practice—that showed great leadership by staying calm and finding a solution together." These affirmations help them understand that their ability to manage challenges inspires others.

Model Conflict Resolution: Share how you approach and resolve disagreements in your own life. Whether it's handling a difficult conversation at work or addressing a misunderstanding with a friend, explain how you stay composed and focus on solutions. Showing them how you navigate challenges reinforces the behaviors you want them to adopt.

BALANCING HUMILITY WITH CONFIDENCE

True leadership is rooted in a delicate balance between confidence and humility. Confidence empowers your child to take initiative and trust in their abilities, while humility ensures they remain open to growth and appreciative of the contributions of others. In the world of Jiu-Jitsu, this balance is especially important—overconfidence can alienate teammates, while excessive humility may hold them back from reaching their potential.

As a parent, you play a key role in helping your child navigate this balance. It's about helping them to recognize their strengths while staying grounded and approachable. Confidence doesn't mean they have to be the loudest or the best, and humility doesn't mean they should downplay their achievements. Instead, both qualities work together to create a well-rounded leader who earns respect and inspires others.

Encouraging this balance isn't just about what happens on the mats; it's a lesson that carries into all areas of life. By supporting your child in understanding when to step up and when to step back, you're helping them grow into someone who leads with integrity and grace.

Practical Tip:

Reinforce Learning Opportunities: Help your child see setbacks as a chance to grow rather than a reflection of their worth. For example, say, "You handled that tough moment really well—what did you learn from it that can help you next time?" This keeps them grounded while building confidence in their ability to adapt and improve.

Celebrate Team Wins: Encourage your child to value the contributions of others. For instance, after a successful team effort, say, "It's great to see how you and your teammates worked together—everyone's effort made the difference." This fosters humility and teamwork.

Model Humility and Confidence: Share your own experiences of learning from mistakes or celebrating successes without arrogance. For example, talk about a time you overcame a challenge by asking for help or recognizing the value of collaboration. Showing them how you balance these qualities reinforces the behavior you want to instill.

DEVELOPING EMPATHY AND INCLUSION

A great leader doesn't just focus on their own success—they lift others up and create an environment where everyone feels valued and supported. Empathy and inclusion are fundamental qualities of true leadership, and helping your child understand their importance will foster not only their growth but also a positive, encouraging atmosphere within their gym.

In Jiu-Jitsu, empathy means recognizing that every teammate's journey is unique. Some may struggle with a particular technique, while others may battle with self-confidence or fear of failure. Inclusion is about actively making space for those around them, whether it's welcoming a new teammate or ensuring everyone feels like a part of the team. Teaching your child to embrace these values helps them build deeper connections with their peers and strengthens the overall sense of community.

As a parent, you have the opportunity to guide your child in recognizing the power of empathy and inclusion. By encouraging them to look beyond their own experiences and consider the needs of others, you're helping them grow into a leader who inspires trust, respect, and loyalty. These lessons extend far beyond the mats, shaping their interactions in school, friendships, and future endeavors.

Practical Tip:

Kindness Toward Newcomers: Remind your child of how they felt when they first started Jiu-Jitsu. Suggest small gestures that can make a big difference, such as introducing themselves to new teammates, offering to help with drills, or simply being welcoming during warm-ups. These actions help foster a sense of belonging for everyone.

Empathy in Training: Discuss how each teammate faces unique challenges. For example, highlight how some may find a particular technique difficult or feel nervous before sparring. Encourage your child to be supportive by saying, "You can do it," or by offering to practice together. This teaches them to see situations from others' perspectives.

Inclusive Behavior: When your child goes out of their way to support or include someone, recognize their efforts. For example, "I noticed how you stayed after class to help your teammate with that technique —that showed a lot of leadership and kindness." Celebrating these moments reinforces the value of inclusion.

PRACTICAL TIPS FOR PARENTS

Support Their Leadership Journey: Encourage your child to take on small leadership roles in the gym. Suggest tasks like assisting with warm-ups, demonstrating techniques, or mentoring less experienced teammates. For example, you might say, "Why don't you help your partner with that drill after class? You've really mastered it." These opportunities build confidence, responsibility, and teamwork.

Celebrate Small Wins: Recognize and praise your child's leadership efforts in specific and meaningful ways. For example, say, "I saw how you helped your teammate with that escape technique—it was great to see you supporting them so patiently." Highlighting these moments reinforces the value of their contributions and encourages them to continue stepping up.

Teach Balance and Growth: Remind your child that leadership is about progress, not perfection. Share examples of how great leaders learn from mistakes and use challenges as stepping stones. For instance, after a tough moment, you could say, "It's okay to make mistakes—that's how we learn and get better. What do you think you'd do differently next time?" This helps them embrace growth as part of their journey.

Fostering leadership and responsibility in your child isn't just about their Jiu-Jitsu journey—it's about helping them grow into individuals who inspire and uplift others in every part of their life. By encouraging their strengths, guiding them through challenges, and teaching them the value of supporting others, you're laying the groundwork for a lifetime of confident, compassionate leadership.

Every small moment—whether it's helping a teammate, learning from a mistake, or stepping into a new challenge—builds the habits and values that define true leadership. Your guidance and encouragement today are shaping the person they'll become tomorrow, both on and far beyond the mat.

"A true leader is one who

knows the way,

goes the way,

and shows the way."

- John C. Maxwell

... and we know, the way is the goal

16. PREPARING FOR PROFESSIONAL OPPORTUNITIES

Jiu-Jitsu has been more than just a sport for your child—it has shaped their character, has become their way of life, and given them a sense of belonging. As they grow, their journey on the mat starts to evolve, extending beyond competitions and daily training. This is the time when they begin to ask bigger questions: *Can I make a living from Jiu-Jitsu? What does it take to become a professional competitor? Are there opportunities beyond competing that allow me to stay involved in the sport?*

As a parent, you have a unique opportunity to help them see the bigger picture. The discipline, problem-solving, and leadership skills they've built don't just stay within the walls of their academy—they are tools that can guide them toward future opportunities. Whether that means earning a scholarship, stepping into a mentorship role, or even exploring a career in coaching or fitness, these lessons have long-term value.

Not every child will pursue Jiu-Jitsu professionally, but the impact of their training will influence them in ways they may not yet realize. This section will help you support your child in recognizing the doors that Jiu-Jitsu can open—whether within the sport or in other areas of life. By being there to guide, encourage, and help them navigate these opportunities, you empower them to take ownership of their path with confidence and purpose.

EXPLORING NEW OPPORTUNITIES THROUGH JIU-JITSU

Jiu-Jitsu can open the door to a range of new experiences for a young athlete. Beyond competing, they can explore roles such as refereeing, assisting in event organization, or contributing to their academy's programs. These opportunities allow them to take on responsibilities, solve problems, and work effectively with others in practical, meaningful ways.

As a parent, you can support your child by encouraging them to explore different roles within Jiu-Jitsu and see what interests them. Some athletes might enjoy refereeing, where focus and quick decision-making are essential, while others may find fulfillment in leadership roles, such as assisting with coaching or event planning. Trying these different roles helps them develop new skills and a broader perspective on the sport.

Engaging in these opportunities allows your child to see Jiu-Jitsu beyond just competition. Whether helping manage the logistics of a tournament or refining their understanding of the rules as a referee, these experiences offer valuable insights into different aspects of the sport. They also build confidence and prepare them for potential leadership roles in the future.

These early experiences can serve as stepping stones for long-term opportunities in Jiu-Jitsu. Taking on responsibilities within the academy or competition scene can lead to coaching, sports management, or other professional pathways within the sport. Exploring these opportunities now allows them to see how their passion for Jiu-Jitsu can translate into a meaningful role in the future.

Practical Tip:

Encourage Hands-On Experience: Support your child in trying different roles within Jiu-Jitsu, such as refereeing, assisting with classes, or helping organize events. Direct involvement will allow them to discover what they enjoy most. If your child is detail-oriented, refereeing might be an excellent fit to help them develop focus and decision-making. For children who enjoy planning, helping with events can build their confidence and foster teamwork.

Create Opportunities for Involvement: Encourage your child to get involved in activities beyond training, such as assisting at a local competition, helping with tournament logistics, or supporting their academy's events. These experiences provide valuable hands-on learning and introduce them to different aspects of the sport.

Help Them Reflect on Their Experiences: After trying different roles, discuss what they enjoyed and what challenged them. Encouraging self-reflection helps them recognize their strengths and interests. Acknowledge the skills and values they're developing through these roles and how they're applying them beyond the mats. Recognizing their contributions can inspire them to take on even greater challenges.

PURSUING SPONSORSHIPS

For young Jiu-Jitsu athletes, sponsorships can be an exciting step in their journey, offering opportunities beyond financial support. While securing sponsorships is challenging, dedicated and hardworking athletes who actively represent the values of Jiu-Jitsu—such as respect, integrity, and perseverance—can create meaningful partnerships that extend their presence in the sport.

Sponsorship is not just about winning competitions; it's about building a strong personal brand. Companies and organizations look for athletes who embody professionalism, engage with the community, and represent their sponsors with authenticity. Developing these qualities early on can help an athlete stand out and create valuable long-term relationships.

As a parent, you can support your child in this process by guiding them toward understanding what sponsors look for, helping them present themselves professionally, and encouraging them to take initiative. Sponsorship is most beneficial when an athlete is already active in the Jiu-Jitsu community, demonstrating leadership, engaging in competitions, and positively influencing their peers.

With thoughtful preparation and a genuine approach, your child can connect with sponsors by leveraging local networks, engaging with businesses that align with their values, and effectively presenting their dedication to the sport. Encouraging them to take ownership of the process will help them develop valuable life skills, such as communication, responsibility, and self-promotion.

Practical Tips:

Start with Local Connections: As a parent, take the lead in reaching out to local businesses and organizations that are familiar with your child's academy or the Jiu-Jitsu community. Your involvement can help open doors and create initial sponsorship opportunities, while your child learns how to engage professionally through your guidance. These connections are often the easiest way to gain initial sponsorship support.

Understand Sponsorship Expectations: Help your child recognize that sponsors look for more than just competition results. Encourage them to align their public image, interactions, and commitments with the brand's values. Professionalism in both in-person and online interactions is key to securing lasting sponsorships.

Create a Compelling Pitch: Guide your child in crafting a sponsorship proposal that tells their story —why they train, what they've achieved, and how sponsorship will support their goals. A personal and authentic approach will have a greater impact.

Build an Online Presence: Encourage your child to share their training journey on social media in a way that reflects their dedication and professionalism. Posting updates on progress, achievements, and positive interactions within the Jiu-Jitsu community can strengthen their appeal to potential sponsors.

SCHOLARSHIP OPPORTUNITIES

Scholarships can provide valuable opportunities for young athletes who are committed to their Jiu-Jitsu journey. Beyond financial assistance, they can open doors to mentorship, training resources, and recognition within the Jiu-Jitsu community. Many academies and organizations offer scholarships to support dedicated students, not only by easing financial burdens but also by rewarding commitment, leadership, and potential within the sport. Seeking out these opportunities can provide motivation, reinforce dedication, and help your child access additional training resources or mentorship programs.

Practical Tips:

Talk to the Coach: Speak with your child's coach or academy owner about available scholarships. Many gyms are committed to supporting dedicated students and may offer financial assistance or guidance on available options.

Think Outside the Box: Scholarships don't always come in the form of financial aid. Some gyms may offer discounts in exchange for volunteer work at events or around the academy, providing a great way for your child to stay involved while easing financial pressures.

Explore Community Programs: Check local youth sports organizations and nonprofit programs that provide financial support to young athletes. Connecting with other parents and community resources can reveal hidden opportunities.

Focus on Values: Scholarship programs value dedication, respect, and perseverance more than competition results. Help your child understand that embodying these qualities consistently can make them stand out as a strong candidate.

By exploring these possibilities, you're not just addressing financial burdens—you're teaching your child resourcefulness and showing them that their passion for Jiu-Jitsu is worth pursuing.

JIU-JITSU FOR CAREER OPPORTUNITIES

For many young athletes, Jiu-Jitsu begins as a passion, but it can also evolve into a fulfilling career. Beyond competing, there are multiple pathways within the sport and related industries that can turn dedication into a lifelong profession. From coaching and academy ownership to event management, sports media, and entrepreneurship, Jiu-Jitsu offers opportunities that extend far beyond the mat.

Understanding these career paths early on can help guide young athletes toward meaningful opportunities. Parents play an important role in supporting their child's exploration, helping them recognize their strengths, and facilitating experiences that expose them to different aspects of the sport. Whether it's developing leadership skills through teaching, networking with professionals in the industry, or pursuing certifications, the transition from student to professional can be nurtured over time.

Career Paths in Jiu-Jitsu:

Coaching and Academy Ownership – Teaching and running an academy allows athletes to stay deeply connected to the sport while developing a business.

Professional Refereeing – Becoming a certified referee can provide international travel opportunities and long-term involvement in competitions.

Event and Competition Management – Organizing tournaments and handling logistics is a crucial aspect of the Jiu-Jitsu industry.

Media and Content Creation – Athletes can build careers by creating instructional content, running podcasts, or working in sports journalism.

Athletic Training and Wellness – Some practitioners transition into fitness coaching, sports therapy, or rehabilitation, leveraging their knowledge of movement and conditioning.

Brand Development and Entrepreneurship – Designing gear, running a Jiu-Jitsu-related business, or developing sponsorship deals can also create professional opportunities.

Practical Tips:

Mentorship Opportunities: Encourage your child to assist with classes for younger students or take on leadership roles in their academy. Teaching builds skills like communication, patience, and confidence, which are valuable in professional settings.

Learn from Role Models: Share stories of athletes who've transitioned from competing to careers in Jiu-Jitsu, whether as coaches, business owners, or media creators. Exposing your child to different paths can inspire them to think about their future.

Explore Certification Programs: As your child matures, research coaching, refereeing, or fitness certifications that align with their interests. These qualifications can open doors to structured career opportunities while deepening their expertise in the sport.

Encourage Hands-On Experience: Look for opportunities for your child to shadow professionals in coaching, refereeing, or event management. Exposure to these roles can help them understand what career paths might interest them.

Support Their Long-Term Goals: If your child shows serious interest in making Jiu-Jitsu a career, help them network within the community, attend professional seminars, and explore potential scholarship or business opportunities that align with their ambitions.

By actively guiding your child's exploration of Jiu-Jitsu-related careers, you help them transition their passion into meaningful professional opportunities. Whether they choose to compete, teach, manage events, or create content, the skills they develop through Jiu-Jitsu can shape a rewarding and fulfilling career.

BALANCING PASSION WITH PRACTICALITY

As children grow more invested in Jiu-Jitsu, their passion for the sport may deepen, sometimes leading to dreams of making it a central part of their future. While supporting their enthusiasm is important, it's equally essential to help them develop a balanced perspective—one that considers both their love for Jiu-Jitsu and the practical realities of long-term career planning.

Passion fuels dedication, but practicality ensures sustainability. Not every child will turn Jiu-Jitsu into a profession, and even for those who do, it's beneficial to have a broader plan that includes education, career development, and financial stability. Striking this balance allows them to pursue their love for Jiu-Jitsu while keeping doors open for future opportunities.

Practical Tip:

Encourage Open Conversations: Create a safe space for your child to openly discuss their dreams, uncertainties, and long-term goals. Ask thought-provoking questions like, 'What role do you see Jiu-Jitsu playing in your life in five or ten years?' and 'How do you think you can balance it with other commitments?' Engaging in these discussions helps them develop a realistic perspective on their future.

Support Education and Career Planning: Guide them in seeing Jiu-Jitsu as part of a well-rounded life rather than an all-or-nothing pursuit. Explore academic and career options that integrate well with their passion, such as sports science, business management, or media production. Helping them find intersections between their interests ensures they have multiple paths to success. Teach them how to balance training, school, and other responsibilities so that they develop strong habits for managing multiple priorities.

Model a Balanced Approach: Share real-life examples of individuals who have successfully merged Jiu-Jitsu with professional careers or academic pursuits. Highlight athletes who transitioned into coaching, academy ownership, or fitness careers while balancing family, work, and financial stability. Showing them practical success stories reinforces that their passion doesn't have to come at the expense of other opportunities.

Emphasize Long-Term Thinking: Reinforce the idea that Jiu-Jitsu isn't a temporary phase—it can be a lifelong practice that evolves alongside their career and personal life. Encourage them to think beyond competition and consider how they can stay involved in ways that align with their future responsibilities, whether through coaching, mentoring, or simply training for personal growth.

Jiu-Jitsu is not just a sport—it's a lifelong community. Whether your child continues training, steps into a leadership role, or moves toward new endeavors, the relationships and experiences built through Jiu-Jitsu will always be part of them. The academy, their teammates, and the lessons learned on the mat create a foundation that extends far beyond their competitive years.

Staying connected to this community provides continuous inspiration, support, and opportunities for growth. Whether through training, mentoring, or simply maintaining the friendships formed, Jiu-Jitsu remains a valuable part of their identity.

Practical Tip:

Encourage Continued Involvement: If their priorities shift, remind them that Jiu-Jitsu doesn't have to be all or nothing. They can stay involved by attending open mats, supporting teammates, or volunteering at events.

Recognize Their Contributions: Take time to reflect on how they have influenced their Jiu-Jitsu community—whether through mentoring, helping teammates, or creating a positive environment. These moments reinforce their impact beyond their own training.

Help Them Find Their Role: As they transition into new life phases, help them explore ways to remain connected. Some may enjoy coaching, others may contribute through refereeing, or simply staying in touch with the community.

Foster Gratitude: Encourage them to appreciate the coaches, teammates, and experiences that shaped their journey. Expressing gratitude helps reinforce the value of these relationships and keeps them engaged in the sport in meaningful ways.

Jiu-Jitsu isn't just about competition or belts—it's about belonging to something greater. Even as life takes them in different directions, the principles, friendships, and support system from Jiu-Jitsu will always be there. By staying connected in ways that feel right for them, they ensure that Jiu-Jitsu remains a lifelong source of strength and inspiration, no matter where their path leads.

"It's not the destination

that matters,

but the lessons learned

and the person

you become along the way."

- Philippe Eggert

CONCLUSION:
THE JOURNEY OF BEING
A JIU-JITSU PARENT

Jiu-Jitsu isn't just a sport—it's a journey, a shared experience of growth that we as parents take alongside our children. We start by watching from the sidelines, unsure of what to expect, and over time, we find ourselves more deeply connected to this world than we ever imagined. We celebrate their victories, encourage them through struggles, and learn, time and time again, that this journey is about far more than competition.

Watching your child step onto the mat for the first time, their belt loosely tied, full of nerves and excitement, is just the beginning. Over the years, you've seen them transform—building resilience, learning patience, handling failure, and embracing the discipline that Jiu-Jitsu demands. And in that process, you've changed too. You've learned to trust their growth, to let them struggle and overcome, to support without interfering. You've come to understand that Jiu-Jitsu teaches more than just techniques—it teaches life.

This journey is as much about us as it is about them. We grow alongside our children, learning patience, perspective, and the beauty of embracing the process. It teaches us that growth isn't measured in medals or belts, but in the quiet moments—the determination to return to the mat after a tough loss, the confidence to mentor a younger teammate, the maturity to accept both victory and defeat with grace. These are the lessons that will last a lifetime, shaping not just their future, but ours as well.

Whether your child continues on to compete at the highest levels, transitions into coaching, or simply carries Jiu-Jitsu's values into other parts of their life, their journey will always be meaningful. The relationships, the struggles, the perseverance—it all stays with them. And as parents, we've had the privilege of walking beside them every step of the way.

Through it all, one thing becomes clear: we are not just raising athletes—we are raising strong, compassionate, and capable individuals who are prepared to take on the world. And in doing so, we, too, have been shaped by this experience.

Thank you for walking this path with your child and for embracing the unique experience of being a Jiu-Jitsu parent. I hope that along the way, you've been inspired to step onto the mat yourself and experience this journey firsthand.

Enjoy the process.

Philippe Eggert

If this book has resonated with you, I'd truly appreciate it if you could take a moment to leave a review. Your feedback not only helps other parents on their journey but also allows more families to discover and benefit from this book. If you found this valuable, please consider recommending it to fellow Jiu-Jitsu parents. Thank you!

YOUR FEEDBACK MATTERS

Thank you for reading *The Jiu Jitsu Parents*. If you enjoyed this book, I would be truly grateful if you could take a moment to leave a review on Amazon.

Your feedback not only helps others discover the book, but also supports my continued work as an author.

Scan the QR code below to go directly to the review page:

or visit:
https://www.amazon.com/review/create-review?asin=B0DWDM44H9

With appreciation Philippe Eggert

Appendices
Recommended Books

For Children:

"BJJ ABC: MY JIU-JITSU ALPHABET"
BY YVES SABRE LEBEH

ISBN: 978-0-9756669-1-3
This engaging picture book introduces young readers to the world of Brazilian Jiu-Jitsu through the alphabet, associating each letter with a relevant term or concept in BJJ. It's designed to make learning fun and accessible for early readers. - Age 5-8

"ROLLS N GOALS"
JIU-JITSU JOURNAL FOR KIDS
BY ROSS KAREFILAKIS

---

www.rollsandgoals.com.au
Roll, Record, and Rise: The Ultimate Jiu-Jitsu Journal for Kids! The fun, interactive journal designed to help young jiu-jitsu enthusiasts track their progress, set goals, and celebrate every step of their martial arts journey. Highly recommended! - Age 7-16

"WAY OF THE WARRIOR KID"
SERIES BY JOCKO WILLINK

This series follows the journey of Marc, a young boy who transforms his life through discipline, hard work, and the guidance of his Navy SEAL uncle. The books impart valuable life lessons intertwined with martial arts principles. - Age 7-14

"Way of the Warrior Kid: From Wimpy to Warrior the Navy SEAL Way"

Marc overcomes challenges at school and in life by adopting a disciplined approach inspired by his uncle.

"Way of the Warrior Kid: Marc's Mission"

Marc continues his journey, learning about setting goals and the importance of perseverance.

"Way of the Warrior Kid: Where There's a Will..."

Marc faces new challenges and learns about leadership and responsibility.

For Parents:

"DISCIPLINE EQUALS FREEDOM"
BY JOCKO WILLINK

This book offers insights into the power of discipline and how it leads to personal freedom and success. While not specific to BJJ, its principles can be applied to support a child's martial arts journey.

"CHAMPION MINDED:
ACHIEVING EXCELLENCE IN SPORTS AND LIFE"
BY ALLISTAIR MCCAW

A guide focusing on developing the mindset required for excellence in both sports and daily life, providing strategies that parents can use to support their young athletes.

"EAT LIKE A CHAMPION: PERFORMANCE
NUTRITION FOR YOUR YOUNG ATHLETE"
BY JILL CASTLE

This book provides nutritional advice tailored for young athletes, helping parents ensure their children are fueled properly for training and competition.

"THE LOW-CARB ATHLETE: THE OFFICIAL LOW-CARBOHYDRATE NUTRITION GUIDE"

BY BEN GREENFIELD

A comprehensive guide on low-carbohydrate nutrition strategies for athletes, offering insights that can be beneficial for parents managing their child's dietary needs in sports.

"RAISING YOUNG ATHLETES: PARENTING YOUR CHILDREN TO VICTORY IN SPORTS AND LIFE"

BY JIM TAYLOR, PHD

Dr. Taylor provides insights into the role of parents in youth sports, emphasizing the importance of fostering a positive and healthy sports environment. The book covers topics such as goal setting, dealing with pressure, and promoting sportsmanship.

FAQS FOR JIU-JITSU PARENTS

What is the appropriate age for a child to start Jiu-Jitsu?

Many academies offer classes for children as young as four or five years old. However, the ideal starting age depends on the child's maturity, attention span, and physical development. It's advisable to consult with the specific academy and observe a class to determine readiness.

Is Jiu-Jitsu safe for children?

When taught by experienced instructors in a controlled environment, Jiu-Jitsu is generally safe for children. Instructors prioritize safety by teaching proper techniques, supervising training sessions, and ensuring the use of appropriate protective gear.

Will practicing Jiu-Jitsu make my child more aggressive?

On the contrary, Jiu-Jitsu teaches discipline, self-control, and respect for others. It emphasizes techniques for self-defense and controlling opponents without causing harm, fostering a sense of sportsmanship and empathy.

How can I support my child's interest in Jiu-Jitsu?

Support can be shown by attending their classes, discussing what they've learned, encouraging consistent practice, and celebrating their progress. Maintaining open communication with their instructors can also provide valuable insights into their development.

What should I look for in a Jiu-Jitsu academy for my child?

Consider factors such as the qualifications and experience of the instructors, the class structure, the student-to-teacher ratio, the cleanliness of the facility, and the overall environment. It's beneficial to observe a class and speak with other parents to gauge the academy's suitability.

How does Jiu-Jitsu benefit my child's development?

Jiu-Jitsu offers numerous benefits, including improved coordination, enhanced focus, increased self-confidence, discipline, and the development of problem-solving skills. It also promotes physical fitness and provides a constructive outlet for energy.

What equipment does my child need to start Jiu-Jitsu?

Typically, a Jiu-Jitsu uniform (Gi) is required. Some academies may also recommend protective gear such as a mouthguard. It's best to consult with the academy for specific requirements.

How often should my child train in Jiu-Jitsu?

The frequency of training depends on the child's age, interest level, and schedule. Starting with two to three classes per week is common, allowing for consistent progress without overwhelming the child.

Can Jiu-Jitsu help my child with bullying?

Yes, Jiu-Jitsu equips children with self-defense skills and builds confidence, which can deter bullying. Additionally, the discipline and respect taught in Jiu-Jitsu encourage children to handle conflicts peacefully.

What if my child wants to compete in Jiu-Jitsu tournaments?

If your child expresses interest in competition, discuss it with their instructor to assess readiness. Competitions can provide valuable experience, but it's important to ensure that the child is prepared both physically and mentally.